A Much Better *Life*

ANDRE A. DUPUIS

PAGE PUBLISHING
Conneaut Lake, PA

First originally published by Page Publishing 2024

ISBN 979-8-89315-583-9 (pbk)
ISBN 979-8-89315-584-6 (digital)

Printed in the United States of America

THIS IS BOTH A BRIEF SUMMARY OF the book and about the author.

Andre A. Dupuis is just an average guy living an average life. He was in his forties when he learned how wonderful life can be. At the beginning of this book, he had low self-esteem and no confidence. As time went on, he learned some of the tools needed to help *build* both self-esteem and confidence.

The stories in this book are of a sexual nature, but are the stories that helped make him who he is today. The tools he speaks of are described in this book. Some are subtle, and others are *bold*. The stories he lived through are entertaining and humorous. When he started writing this book. It was about the humorous stories he had lived through. Then he realized that there were a lot of life lessons that can help people live a better life. He did not write the book as a self-help book, but it can easily be seen as one. Enjoy and have fun.

Like he mentions in the book. If he can make one person see the glass half full, as opposed to half empty, the book will be a success.

IN THIS BOOK, YOU WILL LEARN THE difference between the glass being half-empty and the glass being half-full. Where a positive mental attitude can take you to summits that can be reached when you like who you are. When you have good self-esteem.

The sky is the limit.

I will be using a word I find to be very descriptive: *Oye*. I love this word because you can use it to describe various situations. If you use it once, it's like "Oh…okay." If you use it twice, "Oyeoye," it's more like "Really?" The best part is that you can also use it three times: "Oyeoyeoye." You say it in an unbelievable way like "Is this for real?" I use this word in everyday chats with people. It's descriptive and fun to use.

I also have another thing that I say a lot (to people I have explained the meaning to): *red car, blue car. Red car, blue car* means that we all see things differently. A lot of people tell me I look like Bruce Willis. My ex-wife was with me for fifteen years, and she thinks I look like Rick Harrison from *Pawn Stars*. That kinda proves that we all see things differently. I look in the mirror, and I don't see

Bruce Willis. That's why they sell red cars and blue cars. I like blue, and you like red. So if you read me saying this, you will know what I mean.

Before my marriage, I used to think that oral sex was when you were talking about sex. Boy, did I have a lot to learn. It was quite a while after my divorce that I learned that oral sex was not talking about it, but using your mouth to do it. It wasn't that I didn't do oral, but I just didn't know it had a name. I am French, you know. I learned to speak English when I was nine years old. I was past the nursery rhyme stage by then. There are many English words or expressions I have never heard. I use the "I'm French, you know" excuse for a lot of different situations. I'm going to use the "I'm French, you know" excuse for the fact that I didn't know what oral sex was.

This book is somewhat biographical. It's not a story about my whole life. The first ten years after my divorce were the years when I made up for the years I missed out on while I was in my twenties. I'm just an average guy with a few stories to tell. I'm thirty pounds overweight and bald. People tell me I look like Bruce Willis all the time. That's me.

I have this restaurant that I frequent still today, The Mic Mac Tavern. The owner's father developed his own steak spice, and it's like no other. The steaks there are to die for, and the portions are generous. You don't leave there hungry. I went there for breakfast every weekend up until I moved to Fort McMurray. I would show up there every weekend with a different woman in tow. I was on first-name basis with all the staff there as well as the owner. Best steaks in Halifax.

I will be talking about sexual experiences I have lived through. We all experience pleasure when we are having sex, but the reason I am writing this book is because of the entertaining stories that led to the act. These stories are real and not from my imagination or fictional. I will be using the "f bomb" a lot, but I will be using it as a verb. Not as a cussword. After all, when you have sex with a stranger, you're not making love. You're fucking.

I will be talking about the party side of my life and drug use that led to some of these experiences. The reason I feel comfortable talking about that part of my life is simply because I have never had the addiction that most people experience when they do cocaine, Ecstasy, or MDMA. I suppose I am fortunate that the drugs have never taken control of my life. I used drugs to have fun, for the same reason people drink. To escape reality for a few hours or a few days. *Reality is always there waiting for your return, nonetheless.*

When I met my wife, I was twenty-seven years old, and I could count on two hands how many women I had sex with. I was shy and quiet. I would go to bars and see beautiful women, and I was too shy to approach them. Too scared to embarrass myself. Never really sure what I would say. I had no self-confidence. I would go home and masturbate, thinking about them, instead of talking to them and trying to bring them home with me. I saw the glass half-empty.

I was forty-one years old when I got divorced. Boy, I would have never dreamed of the adventures the future had in store for me. It didn't happen overnight, but I slowly broke out of the bubble I had created around myself. The lack of confidence. The low self-esteem. Once I broke out of that bubble, I would have to say I have been with over two hundred women since. The glass is definitely half-full now. I am having "a much better life."

The difference between me before I met my wife and me today is that I like the person I have become. I am a good person. I do right by others. I treat people with respect, and I find the humor in simple things. I am honest and truthful. Those traits make it easy for me to be a confident person. I am confident, not arrogant. That confidence shines through in one's personality. As does arrogance. People can easily see the difference between the two. Women are attracted to confident men. Not so much for arrogant ones.

Lack of Self-Confidence

WHEN I WAS IN MY LATE TEENS, I had a good friend from school whom I used to hang out with. Kevin and I used to hang out and party all the time. One night we were chatting, and we decided we should go to Cape Breton to go to the clubs there and party. It was a five-hour drive from home. We had decent clubs nearby, but you know how teenagers think. We made arrangements, and the following weekend, off we went. Road trip!

We got to Sydney and booked a hotel room and got settled in. There was a really big club in Sydney called Smooth Herman's. It was huge. There were two levels and a huge dance floor. We went and danced and partied until closing. We had so much fun that we decided we should come back some other weekend. This time, we were going to go back with the intention of picking up some chicks and maybe getting laid.

A few weeks later, we went back. This time we were on a mission. We got a room in an old Victorian-style house. It had been converted into a motel. The rooms were spacious and unlike a typical hotel room. We get settled in and later headed to Herman's. We were partying, dancing, and having a time. Near the end of the night, we start chatting with these two girls. They were pretty good-looking. So we're hanging out and chatting after the club closed down. They seemed to like us. They were both attractive, and I would have been okay with hooking up with either one of them.

We all decided to go back to our hotel and have a few more drinks. We got to the hotel, and we were chatting and getting to know each other. The beds were on opposite sides of the room. After a little while, I decided to go and lie down on one of the beds. Kevin went and lay on the other. One of the girls went and lay with him, and the other came to lie down with me. Things were moving along just fine. We're drinking and chatting, drinking and chatting, and not much action going on. I'm not sure where my mind was, but it didn't seem to be on sex.

All of a sudden, the girls went to the bathroom together. It's a girl thing, going to the bathroom together. They came back, and the girls had decided to change beds. They must have figured that maybe one of us was not interested in one of them, so they changed beds. The one who had been with me went and lay with Kevin, and the other came and lay with me. So we went on drinking and chatting, drinking and chatting, drinking and chatting. Until, all of a sudden, the girls got up and left. That's right. They got up and *gone*.

What the hell just happened? What's wrong here? All it would have taken was for either me or Kevin to make the first move and start making out, and the others would have followed suit. Who knows how crazy it could have gotten? Maybe we could have had sex with both of these girls. Maybe we could have all ended up in the same bed. It could have turned out to be one of the most memorable nights ever. But *Noooo*. I'm almost convinced the girls wanted to get laid more than we did. They changed beds, for crying out loud. They didn't seem to care who fucked them as long as they got laid.

Oyeoyeoye. Talk about self-esteem and the glass being half-empty. We went there to get laid. We get the girls, and we still didn't get it? That kind of scenario would have a very different outcome today. That night could have been a fork in the road for either me or Kevin. Who knows what could have happened after that? One of us could have fallen in love, and it possibly could have changed the future for that person. You know what they say, "Everything happens for a reason." Well, maybe one of the girls would have gotten pregnant. That would have definitely taken one of us down a different path in life. Oh well, let's just say…nothing ventured, nothing gained.

A New Beginning

AFTER MY DIVORCE, I WAS STILL SHY and quiet, but slowly breaking out of my shell. My ex-wife had met a young lad on an online chat room and had been chatting with him on the phone after our separation. So to get even, I went on local chat rooms. I started chatting with a woman. We got to know each other, and I started chatting with another one. Next thing I knew, I was chatting with a third. Ironically, they all lived in Sydney, Cape Breton.

I'd been chatting with these women for a few weeks now, and I was really interested in meeting them. So I made arrangements to go meet them on a long weekend. I was going to meet Mary first, the one I thought I was going to like the most. The plan was that I was going to go meet her on Friday night and spend the night with her. Then I was going to the club with her and her friends Saturday night. I was going to meet the second one, Justine, on Sunday morning. Then I would go meet the last one on Monday before I went home.

I took off Friday afternoon after work. I had made arrangements with Mary to pick up a case of beer and order a pizza half an hour before I arrived. I didn't know what any of these ladies looked like. It was the early days of webcams. I had a suspicion that Mary might be a bigger girl. I had decided that no matter what, I would stick it out and stay with Mary the first night.

Well, I got there, and Mary opened the door. I could not see all of her. Yes. She's wider than the doorway. That's okay. I said I would do this no matter what. I walked in. The house was dark and dreary, and it smelled like a kennel. I'm a pretty clean person and don't do well with offensive odors. She had two big dogs that were penned up in her dining room with a door lying sideways across the doorway to keep them out of the house. It stank of dog. Oyeoye. Looking back, I'm surprised that I stayed at all.

Anyways I looked at her and said, "You have beer in the freezer?"

"Yes," she replied.

"Can you get me three, please?" I asked her.

I didn't even really drink. Oyeoyeoye!

So we were chatting, eating pizza, and drinking beer. I was trying to figure out a way that I wouldn't have to have sex with this woman. I was okay with her being a bigger girl, but a combination of that and the offensive smell in her house made me just want to leave. I was thinking if I could make her have an orgasm, maybe she will be satisfied, and I wouldn't have to fuck her.

Eventually, off we went to her bedroom. I got down to take a look. I was fishing, looking to find her clit so I could try to please her. But no luck.

Then she looked at me and asked me, "Can you fuck me now? I haven't had sex in months."

I'm not the guy who would intentionally hurt someone's feelings. So I climbed on top of her. She was the first woman I was with after my divorce, and I was willing to pass.

We got up the next morning, and she got ready for work. Well, okay.

"I'm off to work," she said and proceeded toward the door. She told me that she was going to be back around four-ish, and she was locking the door, and I had to go. I guess I was kind of a stranger, but I didn't think she would put me out with nowhere to go and nothing to do all day (as far as she knew).

So here I was in Sydney, and Justine was not expecting me until tomorrow morning. I had made plans to go to the club Saturday night with Mary and her friends, but that was not going to happen.

I went to McDonald's and had breakfast. Then I called Justine.

"Where are you?" she asked me.

"I'm at McDonald's," I said to her.

"In Sydney?" she asked.

"Yes! I'm at McDonald's in Sydney."

"You weren't supposed to come until tomorrow," she said.

"I know, but I was excited to come meet you, so I came early."

She gave me her address and told me to give her a half hour to get ready and to come over.

I got to her house, and my first impression was wow! She had the cutest curly shoulder-length blonde hair. Pretty good-looking girl. She lived in a basement apartment, and her place was clean. She had two of the most adorable blond, blue-eyed kids, Ben and Breanna. Definitely an improvement from the night before. This time, I could hardly wait for bedtime. Of course, it's not always about sex and getting laid. I really liked her, and I would have been fine if she didn't want to have sex on the first night. I was definitely hoping she liked me as much as I liked her.

We chatted for a while and got to know each other. I decided that we should do something with the kids and maybe take them somewhere. She told me there was a local animal park and how the kids would love to go. So we took the kids there for the day.

We're walking through the park, the kids were having fun, then all of a sudden, the wind blew in my direction, and I got a whiff of her perfume. I immediately got the hardest erection ever. I couldn't wait to get home and get the kids to bed so I could (possibly) have sex with her.

We got home from a good afternoon with the kiddos. She made spaghetti and meatballs for supper. She was a pretty good cook. It was the first time I had homemade meatballs in my spaghetti. The spaghetti was delicious.

We got the kids off to bed and hung out. I was really starting to like her a lot, and I was so freakin' horny for her. Well, it was getting late. She looked at me and asked me if I wanted her to get me some blankets to sleep on the couch.

The old me thought, *Of course*. I probably would have ended up masturbating on her couch. The new emerging me asked, "Is it okay if I sleep with you?"

"Of course you can," she replied with a smile.

So we went to bed, and we started making out. She was a really good kisser. We started touching and playing with each other. At one point, I had two fingers inside her, and she started calling my name. She was getting louder and louder. *Psh psh psh.* She squirted all over my fingers. I was thinking, *What the heck was that?* She obviously had an orgasm. That was the first time I had experienced that. I didn't even know women could do that. I thought she had peed, until I found out later on that she had actually squirted.

I climbed on top. Penetrating her felt unbelievable. What an amazing feeling to reach orgasm with someone you really like. Now *that* was memorable.

Justine and I hung out for a few months. I brought my girls to meet her. One at a time, of course. She was a fun person to hang out with, and we enjoyed each other's company. Until one day, she decided she and the kids were moving to Halifax. I had to ask her if she was moving to Halifax to be closer to me or to be closer to her sister. Her sister lived in Halifax. She was moving to be closer to me. I liked her. I liked her a lot, but I was fresh out of a fifteen-year marriage and not ready to jump into another relationship so quickly. She ended up staying in Sydney, and our friendship eventually grew apart.

As for the third woman? I drove by her house and didn't even knock on her door. I didn't really have any interest in meeting her after meeting Justine. I went to meet three women, but I wasn't really planning on sleeping with all of them. I just figured that there would be at least one whom I would like, and that was Justine. So I didn't have the need to meet this third woman.

Really?

I ALWAYS HAD A DREAM TO WRITE some songs and make an album. After my wife walked out on me, I found myself playing my guitar and writing some songs. I ended up making that music CD I had always dreamed of making. As I was working on that CD, I met an awesome lady. Her name was Jesse. We met at the local watering hole, and we started to hang out. We were both extremely wounded from our separations. She had just found out that her husband had cheated on her. One thing led to another, and we ended up having sex.

One night I was giving her oral, and I heard her chuckle. I looked up at her and said, "Is there something funny?"

She said, "I'm just trying to figure out what you're doing down there."

Wow, that was kinda weird. It's almost hard to believe that she was married for fourteen years, and her husband never went down to taste her.

After about a month of us having sex, I could tell that she probably had never had an orgasm. I asked her, "Jes? Have you ever had an orgasm?"

She looked at me with a puzzled look on her face and replied, "I think so."

So I asked her, "What happened when you thought you had an orgasm?"

"Well, I got this giddy feeling inside, and I got kinda lightheaded."

I told her that I thought she was really close to having one, but didn't quite get there. The woman was thirty-six years old and had never had an orgasm. Oyeoye. Really?

I asked her if she felt satisfied after sex. She said that she did feel satisfied. She had never had an orgasm. So she didn't know what she was missing out on. She was satisfied having pleased her man. After all, if you have never experienced an orgasm, you don't miss having one. I had heard of women having gone through their lives having never reached orgasm. But with Fantasia sex parties and the openness of sexuality today, I never thought women today were deprived of such pleasure.

I explained to her that sex was a game two people played. At the end of the game, both players were winners. Both people playing won. No one lost, and the prize was called orgasm.

It became my quest to help this poor woman reach orgasm. Remember now that I was very inexperienced as well. I had only been with a handful of women, but I felt I knew enough to help. I bought everything from dildos to vibrators. Nothing seemed to work. I had a massager I used to massage my sore muscles. I also used it to masturbate every now and then. You know? The ones with a big head at the end to massage your muscles. Well, we tried that one night. If all else fails, go with the big guns. Well, I plugged this thing in and pressed the head down on her clit. I was massaging that whole area, and all of a sudden, I heard her squeal. Sounded almost like a high-pitched mouse kinda sound.

"What the hell was that?" she said.

"How did that feel?" I asked her.

"That was the most unbelievable feeling I have ever experienced!" she said.

"I told you there were no losers in the game of sex."

After that night, as soon as I would show up at her house, she would say, "Okay, kids. It's bedtime."

All she wanted to do was have sex. Sex, sex, and more sex. She was like "I have thirty-six years to make up for. Come fuck me?"

We were chatting after sex one night, and I asked her if she had ever masturbated. She had been brought up rather religious. She looked at me with disgust on her face and said, "No!" As if it was gross or improper to do something like that.

"Well, how are you supposed to tell me how to please you if you don't know what it is that pleases you?"

She looked at me as if to say, "I guess you're probably right."

Success! I felt like I had accomplished the mission I had put before me.

Jesse fell head over heels in love with me. As for me, I wasn't over my wife. Again, I was not ready to leave a fifteen-year marriage and jump right back into another relationship without having some "me" time. Time to heal the wounds of a fifteen-year marriage.

I was focusing on my music, the songs I was writing, and the CD I was working on. She was my biggest fan besides my daughters. She loved my songs as much as she loved me.

One night I showed up at her house, and I hadn't brought my guitar. She wouldn't let me in her house. She literally made me go home and go get my guitar before she would let me in. Jesse was a good woman, but the timing was all wrong. If I had met her later in life, I would probably still be with her. This book would have never happened.

A Life Change

NOT LONG AFTER MY DIVORCE, I MET Brad. He drove a purple Acura Integra, which I ended up buying from him. We became good friends. One day he told me he had a date with two girls. He told me that one was nineteen years old and the other was twenty. He was in his early twenties, so that was fine. He told me not to hit on them because they were "his dates." Both of them.

He and these two girls were going to a rave that night. Brad asked me if I had ever been to a rave and if I had ever done Ecstasy. I told him I didn't like techno, and I had never done Ecstasy. He asked me if I wanted to go to the rave with them. I, at the very least, wanted to experience what a rave would be like, so I ended up going with them. He reminded me that no matter what happened, the two girls were with him, and I needed to make sure I did not include myself in their plans.

So later that night, off we went to this rave. He took his car with the girls, and I took mine. A few hours in, I asked Brad if this was as high as I was going to get off these pills. He told me that I had probably reached my peak, and I was probably not going to get any higher. So I took another one. Forty minutes later, I was like "Wow."

I really liked the way Ecstasy distorted your peripheral vision when you're high. I ended up dancing all night. At one point, I looked over the party and… *Is that my sister?* I asked myself.

Sure enough, my sister and her husband were there. So I went over and said hello.

"I didn't think you liked techno?" my sister said to me.

"Well…I think I do now."

I had so much fun that night. I had never in my life danced that much.

Around noon the next day, the party was starting to wind down. I had made a few female friends throughout the night. These girls suggested we should go to the beach. I love the beach. I was most definitely going to the beach with these three hotties. At least for a few hours.

We did a few more pills and took off. We lay in the sun burning. Then we would go cool off in the water. These girls were very good company and had some good stories to tell. We had a blast. We became really good friends after that day.

Well…eventually, the party had to end. But…but. Okay, time to go home. But…but.

I ended up having an amazing time and had a new appreciation for techno. I had always been strictly rock 'n' roll my whole life up until that night. I really didn't appreciate any other genre of music. I didn't like country, didn't like blues, jazz, none of it. It opened up a new genre of music I never thought I would ever appreciate.

Wow, that was a fun experience. So I asked Brad if there were any clubs in town that we could go to and listen to techno. He said, "There are a few, but the best club is Reflections."

Reflections was known as a gay club. I was rather homophobic and was not really sure if I wanted to expose myself to the things I would likely see there. It took a few weeks, but Brad convinced me to join him one night. So I figured I would give it a chance. After all, I had an awesome time at the rave. Maybe I would enjoy Reflections.

Friday nights at Reflections was techno night, and Saturday nights was top 40 remix night. Friday it is.

It was Friday night, and off we went. I was a little apprehensive, but hey! If I was not having a good time, I could always leave. We arrived at the club, and it was not long after our arrival that I could sense that I was being watched. Sure enough, it didn't take long before I had an admirer. He was watching me and was never far behind.

Brad came up to me and told me that I had an admirer. I told him I was quite aware of it. He would realize that I was straight eventually. The music was so good. I did a lot of dancing and had a good time. Well, the first three times we went, this admirer of mine was there and was constantly on my coattails. The man was actually very attractive. If I were gay, I definitely would have been interested.

Eventually, he realized I was straight and moved on to his next target. Reflections became my regular Friday night hangout. It wasn't so bad. I would be watching the dance floor and see two guys making out and turn away and see two hotties making out. I could live with that.

Well, one night, there was this hottie I could not keep my eyes off. Brad came up to me and said,

"Did you see that smoke show with the brown miniskirt?"

I was like "It's hard to miss such a beautiful girl."

I couldn't keep my eyes off her. We ended up getting to know her. I found out her name was Raylin.

After I had been hanging out there for a few months, I was getting to know the regulars and would always end up going to after-parties or after-hour clubs after Reflections closed. Reflections was a cabaret and was open till 3:30 a.m. The DJs were allowed to play music until 3:15 a.m. or 3:20 a.m., so it was freakin' awesome. I would find myself partying till 7:00 a.m. or 8:00 a.m. And boy, I was having the time of my life, making up for the years in my twenties where I went home at closing time. Alone!

One night I was at the club, and this was the night my life really started to fall into place. The DJ was playing a beat that was unbelievable, and I said to myself, *I'm going up there, and I'm going to dance by myself. I don't care what anyone thinks. I'm going up there and dance.* That's the night I realized that my life could be so much better *if I stopped worrying about what someone might think.* I'm a good person, and I don't care what you might think of me.

After that night, people would walk by me while I was dancing and think one of two things: "Look at that fuckin' asshole" because I was having way more fun than they were, or they would think, "Look at that guy. Let's go dance with him," which happened all the time.

Funny how people are always so judgmental. Once you reach that point where it doesn't matter what someone might think of you and what you're doing, it's like a giant boulder lifted off your shoulders. That boulder had weighed me down all my life. Now it's gone…and I'm still thirty pounds overweight. *Haha.*

I peddled weed a good part of my life so I didn't have to pay for my own. Nickel-and-dime stuff. Never big, but like I said, enough to pay for my own.

One evening Raylin called me and told me she had a friend looking for someone to buy weed from. I told her I would be okay with that and went to bring her friend a five-gram bag. Well, I got there and met her friend Britany. Wow, Britany was wearing sweatpants, and I could see her hips, her beautiful love handles, and I was like "What the fuck! I want to hold those love handles someday! When you're doing doggy style, you can use those hips to hold on to." That's why I called them love handles.

Britany and I became pretty good friends. She was a stripper and used to go out of town to strip. We only had one strip club in town, and she sometimes would work there but preferred working out of town. I told her that if she ever wanted to hang out that I was at Reflections every Friday night. "So if you want to hang, come meet me there."

When I went to Reflections, I didn't like to bring anyone with me because I felt responsible to get them home. I rarely brought anyone with me for that reason, but one night, I brought my roommate Travis with me. Well, around 2:30 a.m., Travis came up to me and told me this hottie named Britany was looking for me.

"Britany is here, and she's looking for me?"

Off I went to find her. She had danced in town that night and had talked one of the patrons into going to Reflections with her. He was probably in heaven, going to a dance club with a beautiful stripper. Well, as soon as I found her, she asked me where my car was. I told her it was out front of the club. She asked me if she could put her things in my car.

"But of course you can," I replied.

We went out, and she took all her things out of Buddy's trunk and put them in my trunk. We went back in and started dancing. It wasn't long after we went back in that Buddy was nowhere to be seen. I bet he left there a little disappointed She was wearing a very revealing blouse. She didn't mind showing off her beautiful body. She was a stripper after all. Everyone could see her beautiful little titties when she was dancing. Her beautiful little titties made me so horny. I love little titties. More than a mouthful is a waste. That's right, she was with me! I was literally on cloud nine. Maybe I was going to hold those love handles after all. I know most guys like big titties. I prefer little ones. *Red car, blue car.*

Britany was twenty-one, and I was forty-five at the time. Tonight, I knew I wasn't going to no after-party. I was going to do everything in my power to take her home with me.

When the club closed, she got in the car with me and Travis. I asked her if she wanted to hang out at my place or if she wanted to go home. She was coming home with me. Un-be-fuckin'-lievable. Woo-hoo!

When we got home, Travis went to bed and Britany and I partied 'til the wee hours of the morning. We eventually went to bed. We were lying in bed naked, and I put my hand on her beautiful body.

She said to me, "Whatsh you doin'?"

I'm like "I'm lying in bed with one of the hottest girls in town. I'm going to fuck your brains out!"

"Oh, okay!" she replied.

We got up later that afternoon, and I took her to my favorite restaurant for brunch. MicMac, here we come. We had brunch, then I drove her home. We ended up hanging out for the next few months. She would call me and ask me, "What are you doin' tonight?"

"It's Friday night. I'm probably going to Reflections," I answered.

"Well, why don't we hang out at your place instead?"

That was a no-brainer. I would rather hang out one-on-one at my house with a sure thing than go to the club. We always had so much fun dancing naked in my living room and whatever other crazy things we would come up with.

One night she called me and told me she was out with a couple of her girlfriends. She asked me if I would I come get her.

"Of course I'll come pick you up, baby."

They were at the Palace nightclub. When I got there, I went in and had a drink with her and her girlfriends. Shortly after, we left. On the way to my place, she asked me if there was a place near my house where we could go for a drink before we went to my place. We ended up stopping at the local watering hole. She was wearing the hottest little miniskirt. She was always dressed sexy as fuck.

We arrived at the local bar. I knew a few of the people who hung out there. We were having a drink, and she asked me if we could have a game of pool. Well, all eyes were on us. All the men in the bar were looking at her, then looking at me, wishing they were in my shoes. All the women were looking at her and, in their jealous thoughts, were wishing they were has hot as she was.

So now we're playing pool. She was all bent over shooting, and yeah, you could see her gorgeous ass cheeks.

My buddy Jeffery came up to me and asked me, "Where the hell did you pick her up?"

I was like "Why do you think I hang out at Reflections? Surely not because I'm gay. Now I'm going to take her to my place to hang out, get all fucked up, and have sex."

Yes. She would rather hang out with me than be at the club with her girlfriends. For the next few months, we hung out regularly. Every time we went to bed, I would put my hand on her, and she would say, "What you doin'?"

I would reply the same. "You're beautiful, and I'm going to make love to you for as long as I possibly can."

Indeed, I got to hold on to those love handles I had wished for when I met her. More than one time. I was on top of the world, needless to say. I was not rich or famous, and I was partying with a girl half my age? I'll take it.

One night she called me and asked me if I could drive her to work. She was working in town that night. So I went to pick her up and drove her in to work. When we got to Ralph's, she leaned in the car, said thank you, and gave me a kiss. Off she went.

The following night, she called and asked me to come get her. She had something she needed to talk to me about. When I picked her up, we went to a park and smoked a joint, and she proceeded to tell me that she had met a guy the night before. She really liked him, and she was thinking about maybe dating him. It was kind of like she was dumping me, although we were never really in a relationship. I could tell she was upset that we would no longer be able to hang out the way we had been. I was definitely disappointed, but I wasn't going to stop her. *Good things seldom last forever.*

She ended up dating him, but it didn't last long. The guy turned out to be a dick. Shortly after, she hooked up with one of her girlfriends' brothers. They ended up getting pregnant and, over the next few years, having three kids together. It was fun while it lasted.

(It gets better!)

Chapter 5

The Grapevine

Not having my daughters around all the time and not having the household chores to do, I found myself with a lot of spare time on my hands. I was sitting around one night and saw an ad on late-night TV for the Grapevine, a phone chat dating platform. It was free for women, and of course, the men had to pay. They had to make money, or else they wouldn't exist. So I decided to try it out. You call and leave a message, then listen to women who left messages. You send messages to the women you want to talk to, then chat live. This was how it worked.

Well, I had no idea what was in store for me. A lot of the women on the Grapevine were lonely. Some were just bored. Some women were looking to make a few extra bucks, and some just wanted to have sex. A lot of the women I met I only saw once. I don't remember most of their names, but some of them definitely stuck out from the rest.

I went on the Grapevine one night and started chatting with someone. Next thing I knew, I was on my way to her place to meet her. We had a few drinks and smoked some weed. We partied for a few hours, and I moved in on her and tried to kiss her. Well, she grabbed me and ripped my clothes off, threw me on her bed, and yeah. No details needed. I think this Grapevine thing might turn out to be fun.

Almost every time I went on the vine, I was meeting women and having random sex. It was like there was no goaltender. All I had to do was shoot, and I would score. It was crazy. Some weeks I would meet two or three different women. Some were just average. Some I had no interest in sexually. I would hang out for a while and move on. Then there were the ones you met and you just wanted to eat them alive; they were so cute. A few times I would be on my way home from the bar after closing and would go on the vine, and next thing I knew, I would be on my way to some chick's house. It was nuts. The ages of the women ranged from twenty to fifty. I did meet some who I ended up partying with more than once. These women tended to kind of fall in love with me. I was like "Let's hang out and party, and if I fall in love, we'll deal with it."

A lot of them would tell me to tear down that wall I had up. I didn't feel like I had a wall up, but I will say that I was devastated when my wife left me. So I guess I was protecting my heart from having to deal with the pain a breakup can cause.

I was on the vine pretty steady for five or six years. Between Reflections and the vine, I was having the time of my life, breaking out of my shell and becoming more confident and seeing the glass half-full as opposed to half-empty. I began to like the person I was becoming. I was never a bad person; I just didn't have the skills I needed to do well and feel confident with women. It was always awkward talking to women, never really knowing what to say without embarrassing myself. Even just approaching them. Now, when I see an attractive woman, I'm all over it like white on rice. I found that if I plan what I'm going to say to a woman, it never works out. If I just let the words randomly come out, I'm golden. Watch and see in other chapters how that works for me. It can work for you as well.

You know, by writing this book, if I can succeed in making one person see the glass as half-full as opposed to seeing it half-empty, it will make this book a success. I can't make someone confident, but I can show you that all you have to do is be happy with who you are and stop worrying about what people might think of you. You are who you are, and we are all special in our own way. After all, Barney the purple dinosaur said so. Oye. I can't believe I just said that.

A Few of Them

I MET BARBIE ON THE VINE. BARBIE was in a failing marriage. She still lived with her husband, but they had been sleeping in separate rooms for quite some time when we met. We partied for a few years. We would always go to the MicMac for brunch afterward. I met her daughters. She met mine. We got pretty close. We hung out regularly and had sex all the time. She couldn't get enough. Then one day, Barbie mentioned something about moving in with me. I didn't feel the same way as she did. I liked her a lot, but I wasn't going to commit to something I wasn't willing to devote myself to.

Meanwhile I was still meeting other women and doing my own thing. After all, you cannot make your heart feel or not feel love. *Your heart decides with whom and when you're going to fall in love.* When it makes that decision, you might as well get on board for the ride. Sometimes it will be as smooth as riding a jet into the sunset, and for others, it will be like trying to stay on the back of a bucking bull. Your heart ultimately decides.

Joy was another lady I met on the vine and partied with for a few years. Of course we would go to the MicMac for breakfast the next day. Joy would have moved in with me in a heartbeat, but again, I just did not have the same feelings she had. Joy loved giving me pleasure. Whatever, whenever I wanted. I would go out on the weekends and on my way home; didn't matter what time it was, if I wanted a BJ or anything else, she would service me. Day or night. All I had to do was call. Of course, I would please her as well. I did things to help her out as well. Take her to run errands, pick up groceries, etc. She literally would have done anything for me. I liked her a lot, but never really had the same feelings she had. Some of you might say I was using her. We were really using each other. I did a lot of things for her in return.

These two ladies were in the few whom I actually hung out with for more than a year. I partied with these ladies for a long period of time and don't really have much more to say besides the fact that we had sex a *lot*. Good old Grapevine.

So I was sitting around the house on this Saturday afternoon. I decided to check out the vine and see if there's anyone on there to chat with. I started chatting with this young girl. She lived in the same town as I did. We're chatting, and she told me how she thinks she's a sex addict. She told me how she had sex all the time and always wanted more. Well, I was not letting that one go. We decided that she should come over for a visit.

I went to pick her up. Her name was Amy, and she had long brown hair. Very good-looking. I was elated. Oh my god! I couldn't wait to penetrate this hottie. It appeared I was able to be with her fairly often if she liked sex that much.

We got to my place and were chatting and liking each other. I'm thinking it's time to go play when my oldest daughter came home. She had moved in to get out of an abusive relationship. Well, they started chatting. They knew each other from school.

Uh-oh. That can't be good for me, I thought to myself.

Sure enough, they got done chatting, and my daughter went to her room.

Amy looked over at me and asked me, "Can you take me home please?"

I could not believe this was really happening. The gentleman that I am, I was not going to try to convince her to stay. After all, my daughter was home, so I was not going to have sex while she's there. Especially with a girl she knew from school.

Man, oh man. Talk about the one that got away. She was ready, willing, and able before my daughter showed up, but I guess she was not going to have sex with a man whose daughter she knew from high school. Just for the record, my daughter was eighteen years old. Amy had told me that she was twenty. Oh well. It is what it is, as they say. Oyeoyeoye.

Let's skip over to beautiful Wanda. We started chatting on the vine and were hitting it off. She seemed really nice, so we decided to meet up. I went to pick her up. She got in my car, and I was impressed. She was very attractive. I looked at her and said, "Do me a favor?"

She looked at me with a puzzled look on her face. We didn't even really know each other.

"We are going to go to my place, and we're going to have fun until the cows come and tell us to go to bed. Don't fall in love with me?"

That may sound arrogant, but was more from the track record of the women in the past and the confidence I had now acquired.

Well, off we went. We did some Ecstasy and had some drinks. I loved doing Ecstasy because I could fuck like a bunny on that shit. In comparison to when I was doing cocaine, it would make me impotent. So I would have to stop doing it an hour or two before bed if I wanted to be able to have sex or sleep.

We had a freaking blast. I didn't count, but we probably had sex six or seven times. Probably more. She was hot, and I couldn't get enough. She tasted so good.

We went to the MicMac for breakfast the next day, and I drove her home. When she got out of my car, she leaned in, looked at me, and said, "I'm going to make you fall in love with me."

So I went home. I went to work all week and never reached out to her. Women do not like it when you ignore them after such a fun night.

It was Friday afternoon, and I decided to call her. "Hey, Wanda, what are you up to tonight?"

"I'm waiting for you," she replied.

"Wow, okay. Eight o'clock sound good?"

"See you at eight," she said.

So I picked her up at eight.

She opened the car door and looked in and said, "Want a blow job?"

I'm like "Sure."

Find me a man who will say no to a question like that.

She got in the car, unfastened my pants, and started in on me. I put the car in drive, and off we went, driving down the road with her head bobbing up and down. We're at a traffic light, and this fellow next to me looked over at me and gave me a thumbs-up. Oh yeah. That's what I'm talking about.

So we got home, and we partied hard. We were really hitting it off, and I really liked her. Around 2:00 a.m., I was lying on the couch, and she was on top straddling me, and she said, "You know what?"

"What?" I asked.

"We had sex seven times since you picked me up tonight."

I said, "Uh-huh. Yeah, somewhere around there."

We probably had sex two or three more times that night. I don't give all the women I'm with oral sex, but when I do, I love the taste of a woman. I was so grateful for her honesty. I definitely could have fallen in love with her. She was smart and beautiful. We got along so well. We had unbelievable sex together.

As we were partying, she told me that she used to be a crackhead and that she used to sell crack. That was it. That's one drug I was terrified of. After that tidbit of information, she didn't have a chance.

The thought of her addiction terrified me. There was no chance I would ever get involved with someone who had that kind of addiction even though she was clean. So we got together. We had a disagreement, and she took off. I would have always been afraid she would fall off the wagon. I wasn't willing to take that chance. I never saw her again after that night. I for sure thought about her though. As I am now.

This one night I went on the vine, and I was talking with this young girl. We hit it off, and she asked me to come over and fuck her. I didn't even know this girl. I was thinking that she was probably not very good-looking to be asking me that.

I knocked on her door, and she answered. She looked like she was barely twenty. She had her own place, so I did not pay attention to what her age would be. She had told me she was twenty. She was actually kinda cute. She must have been really horny to boldly just ask some random guy on the Grapevine to come have sex.

When she opened the door, all the lights were out. She was wearing lingerie, and the only lighting I could see was the flickering light in her bedroom. She had candles spread out all around her room. I went in, and we had a beer and chatted for a few minutes. She reached over and helped me get undressed. I jumped on top of her and fucked her hard. On her back, on her side, doggy style. Oh yeah.

When we were done, she looked at me and said, "Wow, nobody has ever fucked me like that before. Will you fuck me again before you go?"

"Of course I will," I replied. Who was I to deprive a cute young girl who wanted me to fuck her?

We did the nasty again, and I got dressed and left. I never asked her for her phone number. I never ever saw her after that night. After all, there were a lot of other women waiting for me to reach out to them on the vine.

Here I was on the vine again, and I started talking to a girl of color. She seemed really nice, so I went to meet her. She seemed to be a lot of fun, and she was attractive, so I invited her to come hang out at my place. We had a few drinks and got to know each other. Well, you know where we ended up. I took her clothes off, and she took mine off. We climbed into bed. I had never been with a girl of color, so I went down to take a closer look. It's different down here. The entrance to her love hole was extremely pink, due to the color of her skin, I assume. So I was fondling her and was wowed by the difference in appearance down there.

All of a sudden, I heard her chuckle and say, "Are you having fun down there?"

"Yes," I replied.

Then I asked her if I could turn the light on. She laughed and told me to go ahead. Her skin looked chocolatey and full of flavor. I went in the pink to taste. Yummy. We had great sex. You know what they say, practice makes perfect. I was definitely getting lots of practice, and I was learning how to make sure my partner was satisfied at the end of the game.

After that date, I ended up meeting a few other women of color. One night, I had two friends come over. We were partying and comparing notes when all of a sudden, one of them looked at me and said, "Pull your pants down."

I was like "Excuse me?"

"I want to see what type of underpants you're wearing."

Well, that was a first. Needless to say, that was an interesting evening. I am a very honest person, and I make women laugh, so they in general love me, and we always have fun when we hang out. Now I could say I had been with not only one, but two attractive women of color at the same time.

One afternoon I was chatting with this girl. Her name was Katie, and she seemed really nice, so I got in my car to go meet her. Mind you, not all the girls I met on the vine were nice or pretty, but I don' talk about them in this book. There's no entertainment value in those stories.

I got there, and she was outside waiting for me. I was thinking, *What the fuck, that can't be her?* She was outside waiting for me, and she was super cute. *Well, that can't be her.*

But it sure was. She had come outside to meet me to see if it would be okay to let me know which apartment she was in. She had just moved back from the States to get off a meth addiction. She and all her siblings were hooked on it. Her oldest brother had moved back to Halifax to get clean. It worked for him and was able to get clean from the meth, so she followed him back to clean up her life.

We had a few beers and smoked some weed and chatted for hours. I didn't know at the time, but she was dominant in bed. I had never really experienced that before. I was used to being the one in charge.

She eventually reached over and kissed me. Well, I was *so* excited. She liked me enough to reach over and kiss me. The fact that she seemed to be the one in charge had a bad effect on me. I was half-impotent. Here I was with this gorgeous young girl who liked me and wanted to fuck me, and I was half-hard. That was a first.

We ended up having sex, but I was only semihard the whole time. I was hard enough to penetrate her, but that was it. Oyeoyeoye.

I ended up spending the night with her. The next day, we went to the MicMac for breakfast. After brunch, I took her to my place to show her my house. I showed her around, then grabbed her by the hand and took her to my room. I tried once again to have sex with her. I could only get semihard again. I came inside her nonetheless. We ended up hanging out a few more times after that.

One night I called her, and we ended up going out to the bar to have a few drinks and do some dancing. All the young boys were trying to pick her up, but she made it clear to them that she was with me. That made me feel so good.

We got back to her place. I was looking at her, fantasizing about what I would like to do to her.

She looked at me and said, "I'm going to go to the bathroom to change into something a little more comfortable, and when I come out, I want you to call me your dirty little whore for the rest of the night. And when I say anal, I want you to flip me over and fuck me in the ass."

Holy shit! What she said aroused me to no limit, but again, she was being dominant and telling me how things were going to be. The one in charge, so to speak.

She came out of the bathroom wearing a skimpy little outfit. We started to play around, and I just could not get completely hard. Unbelievable! I ended up cumming inside her again, with a semihard penis. She never did say "anal," and I just did not have it in me to call her my dirty little whore. I think the dominance thing made me unable to perform. I have always been the dominant one in bed. Oyeoyeoye.

Not long after that night, I met Cathy. We'll talk about her later.

So I didn't get to hang out with her much after that night. Katey had introduced me to a friend of hers while we had been hanging out. His name was Nathan, and he hung out at Reflections. He was gay. So I told Nathan, "I guess I'll probably see you at Reflections sometime."

I ran into him at Reflections a month or two later, and he told me Katey was pregnant. Whoa…pregnant? So I went to see her shortly after. She said she got pregnant right around the time we were together. She told me that right after we were together, she met another guy, and they had sex quite a few times, and she thought the baby was probably his baby. She said she didn't want anything from me even if it was mine. She wanted the baby and was capable of providing for him or her.

The fellow she thought was the baby daddy ended up getting into a motorcycle accident a month or two later and died. I tried to stay in touch with her, but when I went to see her again, she had moved. She had a new phone number, and I could not find her on Facebook. Nothing. I kinda lost track of her as well.

I saw Nathan a few months later at Reflections, and he told me he ran into her and saw the baby. He said the baby didn't look like me and figured it was more than likely the guy who got into an accident was the father. She had a boy. I have two daughters. Just because Nathan didn't think the baby was mine doesn't mean it was not. Do you suppose I have a boy? I guess I may never know. I tried for a long time to find her, but was unsuccessful.

I'm falling in love. Not with any of these women. I'm falling in love with the Grapevine. Good old Grapevine. I'm not done, and we will return later.

A Totally New Experience

So after hanging around Reflections for a while, I had a routine. As usual on Friday nights, I would get home from work, and having worked all week, I could easily just go to bed. I would break out a little cocaine and do a line. Now I'm going out. I would jump in the shower, do another line, get dressed, and jump in my car. At this point, I was done with the cocaine. I would take a pill (Ecstasy), smoke a joint, and head out. By the time I got to Reflections, the pill would be starting to kick in, so I would do another one and head in. I always had two or three beers when I arrived and drank water the rest of the night. That way I could drive my car by the end of the night.

After hanging out at Reflections for months now, I had made a few gay friends. Well, one night I'm in line at the end of the night to get my jacket, and one of my gay friends is in line in front of me. He said, "Hey, Andre. You're driving, aren't you?"

"I am, why do you ask?" I replied.

So he introduced me to this girl he was with and told me that she came to Halifax to meet a girl she had been talking to from a dating site. They got into a tiff, and the girl took off and left her there.

My gay friend asked, "Would you be able to drive her to find her car?"

So I agreed to help her and go find her car.

She looked at me and said, "Okay. You can drive me, but you're not going to hit on me, are you?"

She was average-looking. I may have hit on her, but if she didn't want me to, I was okay with that.

"No, I won't hit on you if you don't want me to."

She asked me again to confirm that I knew not to hit on her.

"I'm okay with that. If you don't want me to hit on you, I won't."

We took off. She told me her car was on Windsor Street. Windsor Street was only about three kilometers long. It started at Quinpool Road and ended when you get to the bridge.

We got to Quinpool and Windsor, and we drove toward the bridge. We got to the bridge, and she didn't see the building she was parked behind. So we headed back toward Quinpool. Well, we got to Quinpool, and she still didn't find her car, so I told her, "Well, you have two choices, either you jump in a cab and drive back and forth until you find your car, or you can come and sleep at my house, and we'll come back tomorrow in the daylight to find your car."

She hummed and hawed and looked at me and said, "Okay. I'll come, but only if you promise you're not going to hit on me."

I said, "Listen, I have three beds at my house, and no, I won't hit on you."

We got to my place, and I offered her a beer. We were chatting and having a beer, and within ten minutes of being home, she reached over and grabbed my belt buckle and started to take my pants off. Well, so much for not hitting on her.

We went to my bedroom and stripped the rest of our clothes off. I looked down, and she had the biggest bush I had ever seen. I would call it more like an afro. Oye. All the women I'd been with shave down there.

She jumped in bed and asked me to put a condom on. She watched me put the condom on and asked if it was put on properly.

"You're sure the condom is on right?"

"Oh yeah, it's on right."

I got on top of her, and she confirmed with me that I had the condom on right again. I guess she was horrified at the thought of getting pregnant by a random guy. So I penetrated her. I could tell she was really enjoying the fuck session.

When I was done, she looked at me and said, "Can we do it again?"

I said, "Sure we can. Give me ten or fifteen minutes, and I'll fuck you again."

Well, eight minutes later, she was all over me. She put the condom on for me and lay down for me to jump on.

The second time always lasts longer, and she was loving every minute of it. Oyeoye. I swear I didn't hit on her.

We got up the next morning and went to the MicMac. We headed off to Halifax. She looked at me and said, "You don't have to believe me, but you were my first."

I knew she didn't mean her first sexual experience. I was her first real penis? The first man she had ever had sex with. Wow! My first virgin? Surely will probably be my only virgin. *Ever.* But hey…you never know what's waiting around the next corner.

We got to Halifax, and our first trip up Windsor Street, she found her car. I knew when she could see her surroundings in the daylight that she would be able to locate her car. She kissed me and told me how grateful she was for my help. She reminded me how wonderful last night had been to her.

Well, Wednesday night, my phone rang. It was her.

"Hey, what are you doing next weekend?"

"On Friday night I will be at Reflections," I replied. "Why? Are you going to come meet up with me?"

"I may do that," she said.

She never did come.

I had to laugh. She really liked the real penis. I would have to say that she probably went from being a lesbian to being bisexual. That was the last I heard from her, but I know she went looking for more cock after that night. I never dreamed that I would ever have sex with a virgin. Especially having met her at Reflections of all places.

C h a p t e r 8

Dirty Little Whore

This chapter gets a little more graphic. Parental supervision is advised.

So I was at Reflections one night. I was partying hard and decided to go to the smoke room for a smoke. This cute little thing walked up to me and asked me, "Hey, can you get me a half?"

She was asking me if I could get her a half gram of coke. My first impression was *Is she a cop?* She looked too young to be a cop, so I answered, "Yes, probably."

She said, "Do you want the cash?"

"Yes, I'll take the cash. I don't want to pay for it and have you leave before I give it to you."

So she gave me $40, and off I went. I circled around the club. I didn't want her to see who I was getting it from. I get her a half and went back to the smoke room. She came back a few minutes later, and I cautiously gave it to her. She looked at me and asked me where I was parked. I told her my car was parked out front of the club.

"Do you want to do a line?"

I looked at her and said, "Sure. Let's go."

So we went out to my car, and she broke us up a line. We did the lines, and she asked me, "Do you want to get a hotel room and finish this?"

"Well, do you want to go to my place? I have a gram at my place."

"Where do you live?" she asked.

So I told her where I lived.

"Okay," she said.

So off we went. We got to my place and did some lines and had a few beers. We were chatting and getting to know each other. She was really cute, and I was liking where this seemed to be going. All of a sudden, she got down on her knees in front of my refrigerator and started twerking, asking me if I thought she had a nice ass.

"Oh yeah! You have a great ass."

And no, I ain't lying. She had a perfectly shaped, round, can't-take-my-eyes-off ass. Oye. She kept on twerking, and it appeared I was not getting aroused, so eventually, we headed off to bed. Well, we're in bed, and I couldn't get an erection. Cocaine tends to make most men impotent after habitual use, but it had never happened to me before that night. She was a little cokehead and was quite aware of my dilemma. She knew that if she could lift my excitement level up a few notches, I could probably get an erection.

She looked over at me and asked, "What can I do to really excite you?"

I thought about it for a second and said to her, "I want to watch my roommate fuck you."

She asked me, "Is he fat?"

"No. He's not fat."

"Is he ugly?" she inquired.

"No, he's average-looking," I told her.

"Okay," she said.

Oyeoyeoye!

Off we went. We walked into Travis's room, stark naked. I turned the light on.

He woke up and looked at the two of us naked in his room and said, "What's up?"

I said, "Travis. This is Naddy. Naddy, this is Travis, isn't she the cutest? I want to watch you fuck her."

He looked a little confused. He wasn't going to say no. How many times in life do you get woken up in the middle of the night and asked to fuck a young cutie you have never met? He was hung like a freakin' horse. So he put on a condom and started fucking her. Oyeoye. He started banging her, flipping her over, and he's fucking her doggie style.

She looked over at me and whispered, "It's you I want to fuck."

I was stroking my limp cock, and I whispered back, "I know."

He eventually blew his load, and we left his room and went to the living room. We sat on the couch. I lived in an old mobile with a bow-front window covered with sheers instead of curtains. Anyone could have seen what was going on. The thought of that really excited me as well. I touched her pussy, and I felt my cock start to grow. I slid my cock inside her. The anticipation of banging this little cutie was like an hour of foreplay. That long buildup made it feel that much better.

I flipped her over and started pounding her. I must have fucked her for twenty, thirty minutes. Ooh yeah! That was fucking awesome.

We chatted and had a beer and eventually worked our way back to my room. I lay down, and she climbed on top and fucked me. She knew how to fuck in that position, and it felt unbelievable. She was young, but she knew what to do and how to do it. We changed positions a few times, and I eventually came again. It was getting late. I lay back and ended up falling asleep on her.

I used to sleep pretty hard in those days. Anyways, I was sleeping, and I could feel the bed was shaking, and I could hear *vvvvv vvvvvv vvvvv.* I opened my eyes. She had found my electric massager. She was lying on the bed with her legs propped up under my window, and she was using this massager on herself.

"What's the matter, babe?" I said to her.

She looked over at me and said, "I want to get off."

So I grabbed her and laid her down and started giving her oral. I was gently biting her clit and sucking on her and eventually banged her again. A few minutes later, I fell back to sleep. I could feel the bed shaking and heard the massager again. I opened my eyes, and she was lying on my bed. She had wrapped the electrical cord up the shaft of the massager and was using it as a dildo.

"Oh, babe," I said.

She looked at me and said, "I want to cum so bad. I often have a hard time reaching orgasm when I'm high."

I walked over to her and took the massager from her. I put my arm across both of her legs and pushed her legs toward her head as far as I could. All I could see was her beautiful ass and her pink love hole. I started using the massager on her to help her reach where she wanted to be. I enjoyed what was happening as much as she did.

"Oh my fucking god!" she yelled. "Finally."

I reached over to her and gave her a passionate kiss. By then I was rock-hard, so I jumped on top of her and fucked her one more time. We lay down and went to sleep. Oyeoyeoye. That was fun.

We got up the next morning. We went for breakfast, and I drove her home. On our way to her place, she told me that she had a fight with her boyfriend the night before. She decided she was going to go out and have some fun. How lucky can a guy be? The love gods were definitely shining down on me. We exchanged numbers, and I dropped her off in the ghetto part of Halifax.

I got home that afternoon, and I saw there was a new video on my phone. I pushed play, and I could hear *vvvvv vvvvv*. I couldn't make out what this video was. I was turning my phone to the right, turning it to the left, and… what? It was her the night before. While I was sleeping, she took my phone and took a video of herself masturbating with the vibrator. Are you kidding me right now? What a dirty, horny little Wh#^%# Unbelievable. These kind of events are engraved in my memory.

You know how they say that when you die, your life flashes before your eyes? Well, I can't wait to die to relive these kinds of memories.

Tuesday night my phone rang. I answered and heard her say, "Hey, it's Naddy."

"Oh. Hi, babe. How you doing?" I asked.

"I'm good. What are you up to tonight?" she asked me.

"Oh, not much. I have to work in the morning."

"You want to hang out for a bit?" she said.

"Sure…I'll come and get you."

She got in my car, and I got an instant erection when I saw her. I looked at her, and she had the cutest curly brown hair. The night I met her, she had straightened her hair. It looked like she had a roman helmet on her head.

"Oh my god, your hair is so awesome," I told her.

She was absolutely gorgeous. She told me that she had straightened her hair that night.

I told her, "I'm not the boss of you, but I don't think you should ever straighten your hair again. You look so much better with those cute brown curls."

On the way to my place, she asked me if I ever heard of a golden shower. I told her I had heard a few things off the internet. So yeah, kind of.

We went to the house, hung out for a bit, and ended up in bed. I got done missionary style and got up on my knees. I was looking at her, and all of a sudden, I see a stream of urine shooting toward me. It was coming in my direction and hit me on my belly. It smelled of urine, and I kinda gagged and almost puked in my mouth. It was all I could do not to get sick. Meanwhile, I was thinking about my bedsheets. My mattress absorbing this cutie's urine. Oyeoyeoye. Really? Yeah…not for me. Did not turn me on at all. Maybe before I had an orgasm? Probably not.

If we planned the act, I may have enjoyed more. What a dirty little whore. I say that in memory of my possible baby mama. I loved it.

Looking back now, I still think about her every now and then. Kinda hard not to. Wouldn't you agree? The thrashing of that massager in and out of her pussy. Oyeoyeoye.

Weekend Love Affair

So it was Friday night, and it had been snowing since three o'clock in the afternoon. There's like twelve to thirteen inches of fresh snow on the ground. My youngest daughter was supposed to come spend the weekend with me. She was an hour away, so I called her, and we decided to wait till the next day for her to come. I was bored. I was not going to go to Reflections tonight, so I decided to go on the Grapevine. I started talking to this lady. She was a few years younger than I was. I was used to partying with much younger women. Anyways, we were hitting it off. We seemed to have a lot in common. She convinced me to go to the liquor store and pick up a bottle of her favorite wine, despite the weather, and come over for a drink.

Off I went on another adventure. She had told me which area she lived in and said, "When you see a bus shelter, turn right just before it."

I got to where I thought she was talking about. There was so much snow on the ground. I saw the bus shelter I thought she had mentioned, and I turned right just before it. *Bing bang!* I ran over a curb and realized there was no street there. Oye!

I slowly backed out back onto the road. I was lucky I didn't get hung up and get stuck. It may have taken quite a while to get a tow truck in that weather.

I drove a little farther, and there was the right bus shelter. I got to her place and went in. She was a pretty attractive lady.

"Hello, I'm Ronda," she said.

"Well, how are you? I'm Andre."

I handed her the wine she requested, and we started having a few drinks and smoked a couple of doobies. We were really enjoying each other's company. She had a guitar, so I played a few songs for her. She had a karaoke machine, so we took turns and sang some songs. She sang and danced for me. I was thinking, *I can't wait to fuck her.*

As the night went on, she asked me if I was hungry.

"Sure, I could probably have a bite."

She reached in her fridge and pulled out some leftovers and warmed them up. She grabbed the plate and invited me in her dining room. She had a beautiful house. Her dining room table was big enough for an army. So we went in the dining room with one plate and one fork. I'm like, *Okay?* She took a bite, then scooped up another bite and aimed it at me.

Oh my god! She's feeding me? How sexy is that? And kinda romantic.

We were getting pretty fucked up, having a good time. It was getting pretty late, and she ushered me to her living room. She had a fireplace and proceeded to light a fire. She went in her hallway closet and pulled out a single mattress and laid it on the floor in front of the fire. Wow. She certainly knew how to entertain her company.

We lay down and chatted some more. I started touching her. We started making out. Kissing is so amazingly arousing. The sex was rather quick and tame, but nonetheless, memorable. It was still snowing all the while.

We got up the next morning, and it's a beautiful day. The sun was shining, and there's like almost two feet of fresh snow. We had breakfast, and she looked over at me and said, "Well, I had a great time last night. You're really fun to hang out with. You know, there's no reason why you can't stay again tonight."

I decided it was a good idea. Meanwhile, I had to call my daughter and make sure she was okay with waiting for the following weekend to come for a visit. I called her. I didn't tell her what was going on, but she was okay with waiting until the next weekend to come over.

I went out and shoveled her driveway. Boy, she had a long driveway, and the snow was pretty deep. I came in after an hour or more of shoveling, and she looked at me and said, "I made you a drink. Take a break, and maybe you could shovel off my deck in the back?"

I stared over at her.

She piped up and said, "If you shovel off the back deck, maybe we can go in my hot tub later?"

Hot tub? Oh yeah. That's a for sure. I had never been in a hot tub outside in the snow.

I shoveled off her back deck, then we hung out and had some more drinks and doobies. She was on disability since she found out she had MS. She had been working for Revlon when she found out she was sick, so she was doing well financially, even though she was on disability.

Evening came around, and she suggested we change and go have a few drinks in the hot tub. I rolled a few joints, and she made crantinis, martinis made with cranberry juice.

Oh man! We didn't even bother with clothes! We went into the hot tub with joints, drinks, and cigarettes. She had a rounded table in the shape of the tub. We were hanging in the hot tub, smoking joints and drinking. I remember the ashtray and drinks sliding around on the bench from the snow and ice. The steam was crazy coming off the tub. She had a privacy fence up, so no one could see what we were doing.

I was in a hot tub in the snow with a beautiful woman, partying. Of course, you know what else we probably did in this hot tub. Oyeoyeoye! What a beautiful world.

We eventually went back in the house.

"That was absolutely freakin' awesome," I said to her.

That was the first and possibly the last time I will ever be in a hot tub in the snow, with joints, drinks, and a beautiful woman. This weekend was unbelievable so far.

We did some more singing on her karaoke machine and partying. Needless to say, when we went to bed that night, we made up for the quickie the night before. We had gotten to know each other pretty good. Sex is so much better in these cases. This adventure was definitely one of the most memorable to date. We exchanged phone numbers and decided we should hang out again sometime.

I went home on Sunday evening. This was one of the few times I did not take my sex partner to the MicMac.

Two weeks later, I was on my way home from the bar, and my phone rang. It was her wanting me to come over and bring her a Big Mac. I stopped and got her Big Mac and went over to her place. She had been partying with some of her girlfriends that night, and they had fallen asleep, so she decided to call me. She ate her Big Mac, and then we went into her room. It was my turn to eat. That night was the last night we ever had sex.

Soon after I met Cathy, and she met a guy she ended up dating for years. We were very good friends for many years after that weekend. The only woman I stayed in touch with out of all the women I had met in that ten years of partying.

I don't know how many of you remember the TV show called *Fantasy Island*. For the few of you who may not, it was a show where you paid money to go to this island, and you got to live out any fantasy you may have. If I were a customer and asked to live out an amazing weekend with a beautiful woman, I can't imagine a more amazing weekend ever! I ended up writing a song about that weekend. How Mr. Rork and Tattoo came to me. How she sang and danced for me. How she fed me. I bet you can guess what the name of that song was. That's right, "Weekend Love Affair."

She has since passed on due to her MS. We were friends to the end.

I miss you, my friend!

Dear Alcohol

I WAS DOWN IN THE DUMPS ONE Friday night, and I went on the vine. I went on at nine, and there was no one to chat with. I went back on at ten. Still, no one was on. I went on every hour until 2:00 a.m. It was going to be my last attempt before I was going to go to bed. Well, I started chatting with this girl. She'd been partying and had a buzz on. I was bored and was looking for some fun. We decided that I was going to come get her, and we were going to go to Timmy's to have a coffee. We were going there to see if we liked each other. If we did, we were going to get a hotel room and hang out.

I went to pick her up and was pleasantly surprised. She was pretty good-looking. We took off, and as we got to the nearest intersection, she looked at me and said, "There's a hotel right there."

No need to go to Timmy's! She liked me already. She went on the vine to see if she could get laid, I assume. Why else would she be on the vine at that time of the night? Well, guess what? I was on there for the same reason.

On my way to pick her up, I stopped and bought two boxes of condoms. There were three condoms in each box.

We checked into the hotel and had a few beers while we got to know each other. We chatted for at least an hour before I went over to her and reached over to her with my hand held out. She grabbed my hand, and I walked her over to the bed. We got undressed. I put a condom on, and we got to know each other a lot better. She was extremely vocal in bed. Just touching her made her react.

We got up and had another beer and smoked another joint and went back to bed for round two. After the first box of condoms was gone, I grabbed her by the hand and walked her into the bathroom. I turned the shower on. We got in, and I washed her hair, washed her body, and she followed suit. She then proceeded to wash me. We continued to chat and have sex. The last two times we had sex, I had to go bareback because I ran out of condoms.

Let's talk about red flags for a sec. I had to get her home before eleven because her daughters were coming over for the weekend. That's right. A mom who was no longer raising her daughters. How big of a red flag do you need?

I got her home, and she wouldn't go in her apartment. She stayed in my car until ten after eleven, and her kids were supposed to arrive at eleven. She didn't want the night we had to end. I felt the same way. I could have had sex with her for the rest of that day, no problem. We exchanged numbers, and it wasn't long before we hung out again.

Sunday evening after her girls left, she called me, and I went to pick her up. I would have to say, she fell in love with me from the first night we met. That seemed to be an ongoing pattern. That was the reason I had asked Wanda to not fall in love with me.

We ended up dating for a little more than three years. It was definitely an on again, off again relationship. Once your heart falls for someone, it's too late. Your heart is in control. You do what it tells you to do. As I said before, your heart decides. People do crazy things for love. Women put up with abusive husbands because of love. Men stalk their exes because of love. People get into bad relationships because they fall in love before their partner shows their true colors. People even resort to murder because of love. There's no end to what your heart will make you do or make you put up with once you're in love. I'm not going to get into too many details, but I will tell you about what alcohol can do.

Red flag? She turned out to be an alcoholic, and yes, she managed to make me fall in love with her—a task many women had tried to achieve before she came along. I have often asked myself how she managed to succeed where many others had failed. I believe these are the things she did to make me fall in love with her.

First, she was very vocal while we were having sex. When she reached orgasm, I knew. I love when a woman is vocal in bed. It shows they are with you and enjoying what's happening. Even after three years, I would fuck her, and it felt as good as the first time. I would look at her and say, "Why does it still feel so good when I make love to you?"

She would look at me and say, "Because you love me."

She was right.

Second. One night we were partying, I told her that my doctor had told me I had emphysema. She went over and grabbed both our packs of cigarettes. She looked at me and said, "We're done!"

I replied, "We're done what?"

"We are done smoking."

"Hold on now. I'm drinking, and I'm going to smoke. At least for the rest of the night."

She actually quit smoking for over a year because I had emphysema. I would still sneak one here and there when I could. But for the better part, I was only smoking one or two cigarettes a day.

The last thing that I can attribute to how she made me fall in love with her was one night, we went to a nightclub. It was rather quiet there that night. There might have been thirty or forty people there, but we didn't care. We had a few drinks and danced and had a great time. Well, when we were at our table, I would be sitting at the table, and she was standing behind me with her hand on my shoulder as if to say, "This is my man!" I can't deny, it made me feel special.

As I got to know her better, I realized that she was not the same person when she was drinking. She was angry and hateful. I will give you a few examples, then we'll move on.

One night, we both had a pretty good glow on, and all of a sudden, she's angry. She picked up a steak knife and started chasing me around the kitchen, wanting to stab me. So I grabbed her wrist, which was holding the knife. I was two hundred pounds, and she was 120. I could restrain her quite easily. Even drunk, I had the presence of mind. Here we were struggling with a knife, and I realized somebody was going to get hurt. Then someone else will be going to jail.

So I let her go and put my hands in the air and said, "Here. You want to stab me? Go ahead."

She threw the knife in the sink. Phew, that could have been bad.

A lot of people black out when they drink. Then they claim they don't remember what happened the night before. Well, this is real. She was one of those people. She could easily have stabbed me and found out the next day what she did.

Another example. One night we're at Reflections with another couple we used to hang out with all the time. I looked at the dance floor and saw this smoke show. I looked over at Mac and whispered, "Check out that hottie on the dance floor with the blue miniskirt."

Next thing I knew, I saw a beer bottle fly by my head. I'm not sure how she heard me, but she did. The bouncer saw what happened. All the bouncers there knew me very well. I was a regular at Reflections. He came over and asked if everything was okay. He also asked if I wanted him to throw her out. I agreed that it was probably a good idea to put her out. I knew the rest of the night would be a shit show, so he escorted her out of the club. He came back and said that she was going to be outside waiting for us. I gave him twenty dollars and asked him to go give it to her and to tell her to go home. She didn't, and of course, she was waiting for us when we came out. I could go on and on about what happened after that, but I won't. I know.

Maybe I shouldn't have been looking at other women, but that's all I was doing. On the other hand, I would go to the bathroom and come back, and she would be dancing with a complete stranger. She could do whatever she wanted, but I couldn't even look at another woman.

I will say something else about our sex life. The girl never ever said no to me. *Ever*. She would put out any and every time I wanted sex. More than once I would wake her up in the middle of the night to fuck her, and she would either enjoy it or tell me to go ahead and hurry up. One time she had the flu, and I thought she would never let me fuck her feeling the way she did. So I woke her up, and sure enough, she rolled over, spread her legs, and let me fuck her. If I went longer than three days without fucking her, she would say, "Are you cheating on me?"

"Of course I'm not. We're always together," I would answer.

"Well, you haven't fucked me in three days," she would say to me.

We had sex as often after three years as we did in the first few months of our relationship. One time she did say no, it was short-lived. We were in the car in Halifax, and I looked over at her and said, "Cathy…take your pants off?"

She looked at me and told me that she didn't want anyone to see her naked in the car. At a red light or at an intersection, someone might see she was naked. *Okay*, I thought. *We could get in trouble if someone saw her naked in my car.*

We got to the on-ramp to the highway, and I said to her, "Cathy…take your pants off?"

She looked at me and started to take her pants off. I reached over and played with her until I made her reach orgasm. After satisfying her, I pulled over on the side of the highway, jumped out, and went to the passenger side. I opened the door and put her seat back. Took my pants off and jumped in on top of her. We had sex right there on the highway, with cars racing by. That was a very memorable fuck.

The first time I had anal was with her. She was reluctant at first, but turned out liking it after a while.

She went to AA a few times, but would always relapse. She could go three months, but that was her breaking point. She tried to stop three or four times, but never went past three months. When I got divorced, I knew I would never be number one in a woman's life because most of the women I would meet would have children. Cathy did love me. I knew that in my heart. But in this case, I wasn't coming second to children. I was coming second to alcohol. I was okay coming second to a woman's children, but not second to alcohol. She simply loved alcohol a little more than she loved me.

I apologize for the change in theme, but I did meet her on the Grapevine, and I did spend three years of my life believing that she could change. *People don't change.* As much as we believe in our hearts that we can help them be a better person, they don't. In a lot of cases, they just can't. Addictions are hard to overcome.

FUCK YOU!

Oops. I'm not talking to you. That is my response to "Dear Alcohol." I may occasionally do drugs, but alcohol is by far the worst drug on this planet. Find me a man who's going to smoke a joint and go home and beat his wife and rape his daughter. There's a reason prohibition came and went. It was definitely a toxic relationship, but I learned to get past the anger.

Longest Labor Day Weekend Ever

THE SUMMER WAS WINDING DOWN, AND LABOR Day was coming up. I love roller coasters and have gone to Canada's Wonderland many times with my daughters. I decided I would like to go spend Labor Day weekend at the park without children. I wanted one of my chickie friends to come with. So I picked up my phone and started calling.

"I'm busy that weekend."

"I already have plans."

"Roller coasters make me sick."

"I'm scared to go on roller coasters."

I got every excuse in the book. A lot of them already had plans because Labor Day was the last long weekend of the summer. Well, I was down to the last number in my phone. It was Jane. I met Jane at Reflections and had seen her at after-parties I had gone to. I didn't know her very well, but a few of the boys had hooked up with her and said she was fun to hang out with, and she loved to have sex. So I called her. She told me that she was already in Toronto, and she was going to be leaving just as I was planning on coming. So I asked her if she would be willing to stay a few more days and come to Wonderland with me. She told me that she loved roller coasters, and sure, she'd cancel her flight and come to the park with me. Then she could drive back to Halifax with me and help me drive back.

Jane was Lebanese, I believe. Dark complexion. Drop-dead gorgeous. Wow. No need to say that I was ecstatic. I was going to Wonderland with a beautiful woman for four days.

It was now Wednesday. Departure day. I was packed and ready to go. I went to work, and when I got off, I was on the highway. I got to Toronto Thursday evening and called Jane. She gave me the address, and I went to pick her up. She was all mine for the next four days.

We went to the liquor store and got settled in our hotel. We had a few drinks, and I was done. I had been up for two days. I cuddled up to her, and I was gone.

I woke up the next morning, and she had slept on the other bed in the room. Hmm? Okay. We went for break-fast, and off we went to Wonderland. We had a freakin' blast. She convinced me to go on a ride that I had decided I would never get back on. It was like the pirate ship that swings back and forth, except this one went all the way around. Oye! I reluctantly got on with her, and it wasn't as bad as it was the first time. I suppose the first time I got on that ride, there was a lady and her daughter sitting beside me. The daughter screamed the whole ride, yelling, "Let me off! Stop the ride. Let me off!" On and on till the ride came to a stop. It was stressful, and I had decided I was never getting on that ride again, but Jane was so hot, and I didn't want to be a pussy. It was definitely more enjoyable without someone yelling bloody murder the whole time.

We went back to the hotel and started partying. We did a few lines and had some drinks. As the night went on, I could kinda tell that she didn't seem to have interest in me, so I looked at her and asked her, "You're not into me, are you?"

She looked at me and replied, "Not really."

Oyeoyeoye.

I was going to be with her for four days and not going to be able to fuck her? I was disappointed, to say the least. It wasn't the end of the world.

I looked at her and said, "That's okay. I'll still pay for everything like I said I would. Let's have some fun."

We decided we would go to Wonderland again the next day. Then we would leave there and go to Niagara Falls for the night on Friday. Then return Saturday and go back to the park.

We went to the park again on Friday and got on a bunch of different rides. It was always a blast at the park. We went for a bite and, off we went to Niagara. We found a hotel and got settled in.

Jane looked at me and said, "You should go to the liquor store and get us a 40 oz. of rum."

We could see the liquor store from our room, so we ordered room service, and I took off to the liquor store. It was one block away, so I decided to walk there. As I was walking there, I saw this perfect little building lot. It was fenced in. The whole lot had beautiful green grass with a small tree in the middle. Aw, what a perfect little building lot. I went and picked up the bottle and started back.

I won't deny I was disappointed that we were not having sex. So I cracked the bottle and had a drink. Then another and another. Then I got to that little lot. I sat down beside the little tree and had a few more drinks. By the time I got back, the food had arrived. I never drink liquor that way. I had a pretty good glow on. I proceeded to eat what was probably the best chicken Caesar salad I had ever eaten.

We chatted a bit about what we should do that night. Then I made the mistake of lying down on the bed. By the time I woke up, it was midnight, and the radio on the nightstand beside me was on full blast. So I turned the volume down. It was probably her last-ditch effort to try to wake me up.

"Jane? Jane?"

Nothing.

She was gone. I called. No answer. I texted. No reply. So I did a line and jumped in the shower, expecting her to respond while I was showering. I got out and got dressed. Did another line. I figured even if I didn't hear from her, I could go out to a club by myself. No word from Jane.

I went down to the falls and smoked a joint. I was still calling and texting. Nothing. Oyeoyeoye. I went back up to the hotel to have a drink in the little bar that was in the hotel. I did a pill (Ecstasy) and figured I would call a cab and go dancing somewhere. I came to find out it's last call, and there was nowhere in Ontario that you can get a drink after 2:00 a.m. Really? Now I was high as fuck, and I had nowhere to go?

The casino was open twenty-four hours, so I went. I didn't gamble as a rule, but I did play poker. I didn't go on vacation to go play poker, but I really didn't have anywhere else to go. So I took out $200 and sat down. I played my first hand, and it cost me $60. I thought, *I have to make sure that I win the next hand I play.*

Well, it didn't matter what I did. I was golden, hitting almost every hand I played. I was building $100 chip stacks. I had two stacks and was working on my third. A clean stack has twenty chips, so each stack was $2,000. Meanwhile, throughout the night, I had been telling the boys at the table how I was with a beautiful girl, and she was not into me and won't have sex with me.

One of the boys piped up and said, "You don't need her. With those stacks, just get yourself an escort."

The other dude said, "Never mind! With those stacks, you can get yourself two escorts!"

Wrong seed to plant in my head. Well, I was working on my third stack of hundreds and started losing, so I decided it was time to leave. After all, it was 1:00 p.m., and I was supposed to check out at 11:00 a.m. I cashed out for $4,500 and change. Not a bad night.

I get back to the hotel and told them I wanted to stay again tonight. He proceeded to tell me that my room was booked for tonight, and he didn't have a room for me.

Finally Jane called. So I told her I wanted to stay again tonight, but I had to pack and find another room. She told me that there was a party we could go to that night and to call her back later. I went to the room and packed everything up and left.

I went to four or five hotels before I found a room. It was Labor Day weekend, and I was lucky I found a room at all. I checked in, and I didn't have a credit card, so I had to give them a $200 deposit and $150 for the room.

I got to my room, and the seed had sprouted into a plant. I was high, but not on drugs. I was high on the adrenaline from the money I had just won. I opened the yellow pages under escorts. I called and got them to send me a girl. One was enough. I just wanted to get off and relieve the pressure that had been building up.

Knock, knock.

I opened the door, and she came in.

"How much?" I asked.

She told me it's $150 for a half hour. I paid the girl and asked her to start with oral, and I'd take it from there.

She put a condom on me, and as she put her lips on my penis, there was a *knock, knock* on the door.

Who in the hell can that be? Jane doesn't even know where I am.

So I ignored the knock.

Bang bang again, so I asked, "Hello. Who is it?"

"It's security and the manager."

"Can I help you?" I answered.

"We would like to know who that lady that just came to your room is?" they asked me.

I replied, "She's a friend of mine. What is it to you?"

"Well, we think she's a prostitute, and we would like her to leave," they said to me.

I opened the door, and she bolted. Oye! They went on telling me how prostitution is a big deal in Ontario, and they wanted me to leave their hotel.

No freakin' doubt, she was dressed like a freakin' hooker. Fishnet stockings with a skirt that was showing camel freakin' toe. Oyeoyeoye.

"Okay. Okay. I'll grab my bag and come get my money and leave."

"Oh. We're not going to give you your money back."

"Excuse me. I've only been in the room half an hour. Okay, fine. Keep the money for the room, but give me back my deposit."

The manager said he'd go and see, and the security dude walked me out to my car. I was there arguing how I should at least get my deposit. I was telling him how I just left the casino and won $4,500. I walked to the back of the car to put my suitcase in the trunk, and it was locked. I went back to the front of the car to open the hatch, and I was still arguing with Buddy. Finally, we'd been out there for probably ten, fifteen minutes.

"You're not getting any of your money back," he said to me.

"Fine. I'm gone," I said to Buddy.

I backed up and took off. I called Jane to tell her how I'd changed my mind, and I was heading back to Toronto. She told me she was going to stay and go to that party, and she would take a bus back tomorrow. She then asked me if I would come pick her up tomorrow at the bus station. Perfect. I could go through with the escort thing.

"Sure. I'll come pick you up tomorrow then."

She asked me to meet her at the city limits so she could get a few things out of her luggage. I met her, and she got some things out of the trunk, and I left.

About a half hour out of Niagara, the adrenaline rush wore off. I needed a line to bring me around. I pulled over and went to the trunk. No suitcase. Well, do you suppose Jane took my suitcase out of the car and forgot to put it back? I drove back to the meeting spot. No suitcase. I was done. I headed for Toronto.

I got to the hotel in Toronto and opened the yellow pages. Asian escorts. I picked up the phone and told Buddy where I was. Then I told him that I wanted a girl in her twenties, and if she's not cute, I was not letting her in. Then I told him to tell her to call when she got here, and I would come down and let her in the side door.

Twenty minutes later, she called, and I went down to let her in. She was a cute little Chinese girl who barely spoke any English. We went up, and I paid her $150. She was cute, and I was bustin' a nut by now. I was pounding this girl, and she was loud. Like really loud. I'm fucking her doggie style, and her face was pointing at the wall to the next room. I was thinking, *Holy shit! She's so loud, I'm going to get kicked out of this hotel too.*

Finally, the pressure was released. She went into the bathroom to clean up and came back out telling me how she liked me and I was a nice man. She ended up giving me oral before she left. *Bonus!*

The boys planted the seed that had then grown into a tree, but mission accomplished. It wasn't cheap though. Let's see.

I spent

- $200 for deposit;
- $150 on the first room;

- $150 on the escort who got me kicked out;
- $150 in the new hotel;
- $150 on the other escort;
- $170 going to Walmart and buying new clothes, toiletries, and a suitcase;
- $200 on the drugs I had left in my suitcase.

Total: $970.

If you subtracted what it should have cost me, $150 for the room and $150 for the escort, $300, so it cost me $670 to get laid.

It was worth it though. That young Chinese girl was fun to bang. If I hadn't won all that money at the casino, none of these shenanigans would have happened. I was ready for some sleep.

I got up, and off I went to Walmart. I realized by then that I had left my suitcase at that hotel in Niagara, so I called.

"No, we don't have a suitcase in the lost and found, and no one turned one in," they said to me.

I hung up. Of course no one turned one in. I had told that security dude about my winnings at the casino. So as soon as I left, he grabbed the suitcase that I had left sitting behind my car. He put it in his car, hoping that the money would be in it. The only thing in the suitcase was my clothes and what I had left for drugs. Probably like two grams of coke and a few pills.

I called Jane. I went to pick her up later, and off we went back to Wonderland for the last time. While we were at the park, Jane got a call inviting us to a rave that was happening in Toronto Sunday night. Jane knew people all over Ontario as she had lived there for years before she moved to Halifax. Perfect, one last blast before we headed home.

We left the park and headed for Toronto. We got a hotel room, got ready, and headed off to this rave. I had a pocket full of cash. I don't even remember how many Ecstasy pills I bought and two or three grams of coke. We were partying!

I was dancing my heart out. The music was absolutely wicked. They knew how to party in Toronto. I heard a techno riff using piano that sounded unbelievable. I saw Jane with this gangsta-lookin' dude. We chatted for a few minutes, and I got back to the dance floor. I was partying hard. There were a lot of Asians there. Asian women are beautiful.

Around 3:00 a.m., I headed outside for a smoke. I was having a smoke, thinking, *I haven't seen Jane in a few hours.* I went back in and started looking for her. I could not find her anywhere. I was high as fuck. So I decided the best way to find her was I would go to the entrance of the club, start on the left side of the door, and follow the wall all the way around the club, looking as I go. I went all the way around, back to the right side of the entrance. No Jane.

I started thinking, *I don't really know Jane that well, and the last time I saw her, she was with that gangster-lookin' dude.* All of a sudden, I was thinking that they went back to the hotel to see if they could find the rest of my money and take it. Oyeoyeoye!

I jumped in a cab to go to the hotel. I got there. No Jane. My money was still there, so I hid it in a better spot and headed back to the rave.

I was dancing my heart out when I heard the angel on my right shoulder whisper in my ear, "Andre. You've been dancing for hours. You better go sit down and take a break, or you may drop dead of a heart attack!"

Then I heard the devil on my left shoulder whisper, "Andre. If you drop dead right now, you will die happy."

I had heard that conversation six or seven times during my party days at Reflections. I'm still among the living.

I started fist pumpin' and kept on keeping on. Well… it was getting late. Or early (depending on how you look at it). It's 11:00 a.m., and I went out for a smoke, deciding that it's probably almost time to go.

I was sitting there having a smoke, and this six-foot Middle Eastern–looking dude, probably midforties, early fifties, came into the smoking area, and he just stood there looking around. He was not even having a smoke. Hold on. This guy did not belong in a place like this. The people here were mostly in their twenties and some in their thirties. My brain started going, *This guy's a cop. He's here to find me! The hotel found the suitcase and opened it up. They found the drugs that were in there and called the cops. So now the cops are looking for me to bust me for possession and for trying to hire an escort!*

My car was parked on the corner of College and Spadina with my license plate sticking out at the intersection, a purple Acura Integra with a personalized plate: ROCK IT. Talk about someone who's easy to find.

I smoked like six or seven cigarettes, thinking, *If I'm going to jail, I won't need a smoke anyways*. I continued thinking, *They don't want to bust me in here because of all the people around, so they're going to wait 'til I leave and nail me then.*

I finally got up the nerve to leave and go find Jane to get the fuck outta here. I found her, and we headed out. I figured I would take her in the car and tell her what I thought was going on.

We went outside and headed toward the car. I stopped and thought, *If the cops are watching for me, I better not get in my car with the keys, or then they can get me for a DUI as well.*

So I lay my keys on the windowsill of the restaurant beside my car. We got in the car, and I told Jane that I thought the cops were going to arrest me, blah, blah, blah. Well, it was time to head out, and what will be, will be.

We were outside, and the cops were nowhere to be seen. Okay…this was good. So we hailed a cab and headed back to the hotel. *What did I forget?* By the time we got back to the hotel, I realized. *Oh my god! I forgot my fuckin' keys on the windowsill.* Back in a cab. Back to College and Spadina. I got there…no keys! Oyeoyeoye.

I looked around, could not find them anywhere. I called where the party was being held and asked them if any keys were turned in.

"Yeah, there's a few sets of keys here," she said.

"Any with a remote?" I asked.

She told me there were three sets with a remote. Thank god! I went in, and of course you know, none of those keys were mine. Are you kidding me right now?

I headed back to the hotel call a tow truck to tow my car to an Acura dealership. Thank god for CAA because they ended up moving my car twice. I hung up, and it's time to get some well-deserved sleep.

My phone rang. It was the tow truck driver. He tells me he couldn't find a spot to park my car at the nearest dealership. So I asked him to take my car to the nearest dealership to Brampton. My sister lived in Brampton.

We got up later that day, and I looked at Jane and said, "It's Labor Day weekend, and the only people who can make me a key is the Acura dealer. They don't open until tomorrow. I'm going to spend the night at my sister's, and I'm going to the dealers first thing Tuesday, as soon as they open. Now listen to me! I'm going to the dealers around nine. It won't take long for them to make me a key. I'm going to call you around nine fifteen, and you need to answer because I'm already going to be a day late getting home for work. So we need to leave as soon as I get a key. If you don't answer…you're going to have to find another way to get home because I'm not going to wait for you."

I went to my sister's. I took her and her family out for Chinese food and to hang out for the night. I got up the next morning, and my sister drove me to the dealers on her way to work. I got my key and called Jane. No answer, so I texted her. I was a half hour from Toronto, so I headed off in that direction.

I got to Toronto, and I still couldn't get a hold of her. I found myself over by the CN Tower. Oyeoyeoye. Okay, I was going to park and give her an hour to get back to me. I had never been to the top of the CN Tower, so I decided to go up and see Toronto from an awesome viewpoint. I will admit, it was pretty cool up there.

Still no word from Jane, so I decided to have a bite in the rotating restaurant that I had heard so much about.

I got there, and one of the hosts sat me down at a table. I was waiting, and waiting, and waiting. No waiter or waitress came to take my order, so I ushered one of the hosts and asked her to get me a server. Five minutes later, a waiter came to my table.

"I'm thinking the Tower burger."

He told me it was very popular and that it was amazing. So that's what I ordered. While I was waiting on my food, I saw my waiter sit this couple at a table in front of me. He was going all out with the awesome service. He brought them wine, pouring it for them, chatting and laughing. Now…I was pissed. He didn't even come to serve me. I had to get one of the hosts to get him for me, and now he was giving them the royal treatment? *Grrr.*

My food arrived, and yeah, it's not my waiter who brought me my food. Now I was even angrier. I started to eat, and my god! That Tower burger was probably the best burger I had ever eaten. The fries were like long potato wedges, and they were awesome as well. Mmm, mmm! That was awesome. So I had like three fries left on my plate, and I was stuffed. I grabbed one last fry. Well, lookie here!? What's that on my plate? A long dark hair. I'm bald, so I knew it wasn't mine. Well, with the service I received here today, I was like "I'm not paying for this meal."

I called one of the hosts over and asked him to send the manager to my table. He came over and had my waiter with him.

"Look what I found on my plate."

They looked down and then looked at my bald self. I proceeded to tell the manager what poor service I received in their establishment and how my waiter had to be ushered over to serve me and how he had given the couple in front of me the service that everyone should get when they come here, and now…there's a hair on my plate.

They stood there looking at me as if I was trying to get out of paying for my meal.

I pulled out the stack of hundred dollar bills I had in my pocket and flicked through the stack. "I'm not trying to get out of paying for my bill. I can afford the thirty dollar burger, but with the service I received here today, and now there's a hair on my plate? I'm actually a good tipper if I receive good service." I looked directly at my waiter as I was saying that.

The manager looked at me and asked me what I think he should do.

"Well…I think the burger should be on the house," I replied.

They left, and a few minutes later, my waiter brought my bill. They charged me for the pop. Unbelievable. The waiter asked me if I would like anything else.

I looked at him and said, "You know what? After all this, I think I'll have a beer."

He brought my beer. I drank it, paid my bill, and disappeared. Well, it was about 11:30 a.m. now, and I still hadn't heard from Jane.

I left the tower and saw a lady sitting on a bench. I strutted on over and lit a cigarette. I started chatting with this lady and told her what's going on. How I had told Jane to make sure she answered her phone at nine fifteen and how it was almost lunch, and I was still waiting.

"What would you do?" I asked the lady.

She told me that if she was me, she would leave. Perfect! Decision made. I was leaving for home, and she can find her own way back.

I got in the car and started the engine, and my phone rang. Guess who? I was over-the-top pissed at this girl by now.

"Hello? Where are you? Text me the address. I'm on my way."

I got there, and she got in the car and told me we had to get some of her things at one of her friends across town. It was a rather quiet drive across town. She got her things, and off we went. Finally.

Jane liked techno and nothing but techno. No rock, no country, nothing but techno, and I knew this. So I put my CD in and turned the stereo on 8 and started singing with the music. She reached over to turn the volume down, and I tapped her hand like a child. No words were spoken. I played every Joe plastic CD I had and sang along. I love Joe's music.

We reached Montreal. I rarely drive through Montreal without stopping for a smoked meat sandwich. I googled "smoked meat," and my navigator took me to the nearest restaurant to have my sandwich. I parked the car and looked at her and asked her if she was going to come in and eat.

She said, "No…just bring me a chicken sandwich."

Perfect! I went in and had my sandwich. It was so good that I had to order another one, along with a chicken sandwich. If you've never had a Montreal-style smoked meat sandwich, you have to experience that. The bestest ever! You hardly have to chew it. It melts in your mouth.

I went back in the car, turned the stereo to eightish, and off we went. I listened to every rock CD I owned and sang along to most of them.

Somewhere past Quebec into New Brunswick, she fell asleep. So I respectfully turned the volume down a bit. Eventually I was getting tired, so I pulled over behind a gas station. I quietly parked and had a short nap. Then I woke up and drove the rest of the way back to Halifax. We got close to her house, and she asked me to go past her house and drop her off. She didn't want her dad to see her getting out of my car.

Thank god that's over! We did have fun at the park. Not so much at the rave because I didn't really see much of her there.

I left Halifax with $1,600 for my vacation and came back with $2,600. Not too bad, considering.

I saw Jane six or eight months later at Reflections. I was dating Cathy by then. She came over and gave me a big hug and asked me how I was doing. I guess she figured out why I had been so angry with her on the drive back from Toronto.

Cathy saw this and came over. "Who the fuck was that?"

"Just a friend. Don't worry! She's just a friend," I replied.

Oh! As for the cop who showed up at the rave? I thought about that for months afterward. I think I figured out what the hell he was doing there. Remember how around 3:00 a.m., I thought Jane had gone back to the hotel to rob me? How I left in a cab and came back half an hour later? Well, it was a rave, and I'm sure the cops were keeping an eye on things. So I figured that they saw me leave and return a half hour later. They thought I went to get more drugs. I mean, who leaves a rave and comes right back a half hour later? More than likely a drug dealer who ran out and went to reload. That was the only rational conclusion as to why he would have been there. I know he was definitely a policeman. He was not there for the music. When he saw me leave, and I didn't communicate with anyone at the rave, they must have come to the conclusion that they may have been wrong about who I was. When they saw me get in my car and ran my plate, they knew I didn't even live in Toronto. The fact that I got out of my car and took a cab, they had no reason to bother with me.

I'm a Lucky Man

As you can see, life is much better when you see the glass half-full. When you are confident and have good self-esteem. It doesn't matter what is going on in your life. My philosophy is that it could always be worse. You can always find a scenario in which things could be worse.

Let me give you an example. Your best friend gets in an accident and passes away. Well, how the scenario could be worse in this case is there could have been other people you knew with him/her who could also have perished.

So I've been living in Fort McMoney for almost eleven years now. I was self-employed most of my life and didn't save for my retirement. They taught me algebra in school instead of teaching me money management. I do not have a pension or money put aside for retirement. So here I was, 5,300 kilometers from the ones I love. I cannot get in my car to go see them. It's hard to be so far from your family.

Anyways, when COVID, hit we got kicked off site and told to quarantine until further notice. Well, I was not quarantining in McMoney. So I booked a flight and went to quarantine with my family.

I was home for a few weeks, and one day I went to Shoppers to get a prescription filled. When I was home, I use my mom's vehicle. She drove a minivan. Here I was (stereotypical), an old guy in a minivan. Probably a family man.

I got to Shoppers and parked the van, and as I was getting ready to go in, this black Camaro with two silver racing stripes pulled in beside me. *Oooh. Nice car*, I thought. I looked in the car and saw a beautiful young lady. *Oooh. Nice girl.*

Masks were mandatory, and I was using a bandana. My bandana had a skull design, and it matched up to my face. I got out of the car, and this young lady came around the corner of her car. I pulled my bandana up over my face and looked over to her and said, "This is a stickup. Give me your car keys!"

She looked at me and started to laugh. We started chatting, and I told her I was home because of COVID and that I lived in Fort McMoney. We were chatting about this and that, and finally we headed in to do our thing.

Oh my god, she's fucking gorgeous! And she's super friendly! If I don't talk to her again, I'll never see her again.

So I was eyeballing shoppers looking for her, and out she came from one of the aisles. I strutted on over and started chatting with her again. We were hitting it off like we were old friends.

All of a sudden, she piped up and said, "You should come over for a beer!"

"When?" I asked.

"I just bought a case of beer. Now," she said.

"Okay. Well, Mom made steak for supper. So let me go have supper, and I'll be over after we eat."

So we exchanged numbers, and off we went. Mom did have steak for us, but I also wanted to have a shower and wanted to pick up a couple grams of coke, just in case. By the way she was talking, I had a feeling that she might like to do a few rips. She texted me her address, and I got ready and went over.

We started to party, and she told me how she used to be a stripper, and she had stopped dancing to try to start her own clothing brand. So we were having an awesome time. We seemed to be on the same page.

All of a sudden, the age thing came up. I knew she was thirty-three. I was thinking, *Andre…lie. It's okay to lie. It's only a little white lie. Andre…lie!*

I looked at her and said, "I'm fifty-eight."

She piped up and said, "Oh…my last boyfriend was older than that."

Yes, yes, yes! I was thinking. I have never been able to lie since my divorce, especially about my age. My ex-wife lied to me during our breakup, and it practically destroyed me. I swore after that, that I would never lie to anyone.

We were partying and getting to know each other. Well, around midnight, we had a pretty good buzz on. We were sitting on her couch, and she got up and grabbed a blanket she had on her floor and slid the blanket out in front of me.

I was thinking, *Is she going to strip for me right now? Is this really happening?*

Well, she got down on this blanket and started to twerk. She had the perfectly shaped ass, and she was shaking it for me. Just for me. Talk about being on cloud nine.

She got up off the blanket, took her pants off, and started twerking again. I couldn't even believe what was happening right now. I love the shape of a woman, and she had all the perfect curves in all the right places.

Eventually she got up and came to sit beside me. I was looking everywhere in her house, at the ornaments, the pictures on her walls, the ceiling, yes, just staring at her ceiling. I was looking everywhere, then I turned to look her in the eye and said, "Am I dead right now? Is this heaven?"

She laughed and said, "No, Andre. You're not dead."

"Can you pinch me?"

She chuckled again, and we went on partying. We had so much fun! I didn't want it to end.

Around 10:00 a.m., we went into her room and lay down. As soon as I touched her, I was instantly erect and ready to rock.

We got up later, hung out for about an hour, and I went home. On my way home, I was thinking about how lucky I was and how if I hadn't approached her, I would have never met her, and If I didn't go back to talk to her again in the store, I would have never gotten to know her.

Boy, the world is a much better place to be in when you're confident and have good self-esteem. It can be a pretty dark place (if you let it). *How you perceive things dic-*

tate how things turn out. If you think positive, you get positive results.

I ended up staying home for most of the summer. Me and Arianna partied four or five times before I went back to McMoney. I took her to Hopewell Rocks in New Brunswick and had an amazing time. She let me take a video of us having sex to take back to McMoney with me. She was an amazing person, and we always had fun when we're together.

After partying that many times, I was thinking to myself, *You know, she's absolutely drop-dead gorgeous, but she's not very good in bed.* Then I realized, we always had sex after partying for hours and sometimes days. She probably thought the same about me. So I decided it was time to have sex somewhat sober, and boy, was I wrong. She's beautiful and very good in the sack.

The third time we partied, I got to her house, and I looked at her and said, "You know what would be an awesome way to start the night?"

"What's on your mind?" she asked.

"It would be awesome if you gave me oral before we get all fucked up."

So she took me up to her room and took my pants off and started in on me. Damn, it felt good. After eight or ten minutes, I could tell that I probably wasn't going to reach orgasm, so I got up off the bed and told her to get on the bed, that I needed to fuck her. She threw me back on the bed and made sure she finished what she started. It was quite arousing, her taking charge and making sure I got what I asked for.

So my birthday is on December 22 (feel free to send gifts), and Arianna's is on the twelfth. I'm usually home for Christmas, so we usually celebrated our birthdays together. In 2021, I decided to take her on a trip, so I called her and asked her if she would like to go down south for her birthday.

She was so excited. "Of course I would love to go with you," she said.

So I gave her two choices to make. First, I asked her where she would like to go. I said, "We can go to Jamaica and go to Hedonism II and share each other with other couples and party for ten days, or we can go to Mexico and have a quiet vacation just the two of us."

Second, she had to decide if she wanted to go for her birthday or go for Christmas. We were going for ten days, so we wouldn't be able to be there for both her birthday and Christmas. Well, she said, "Where's the coke the best?"

I told her the coke in Jamaica was awesome. I had been to Jamaica, and it was probably the best I had done in years. In Mexico we all know the cartel operates out of there, so if we get the right contact there, the coke is probably better.

"Well," she said, "you know what? Let's just go to Mexico, and let's go for Christmas. That way we can spend Christmas together."

"Perfect!" I replied.

I thought she was going to take a week or two to think about it, but she knew as soon as I gave her the choices.

I got on the phone and booked my flight home and called Travel Guru in Edmonton to plan our trip to Mexico. He booked our flight and accommodations, and when he called to give me the particulars, he told me that he had a Mexican there who took care of most of his clients who went to Mexico. He would pick us up at the airport and drive us back. He gave me Roberto's contact information and told me that if I needed anything to ask Roberto, and he would take care of us.

So I connected with Roberto on WhatsApp. I asked him if he could get me some coke. He asked me if I wanted the commercial stuff or the cartel stuff. I told him I wanted the best he could get. He replied and told me I would have to buy eight grams if I wanted the good stuff, and it would be $80 a gram. Keep in mind, that is in American funds. Wow, that's expensive. But hey, you only live once. So I told him to go ahead. Arianna would have liked for us to have a girl party with us for one night. So I asked him if he could find us a woman to spend one night with us. He said he would look into it.

We were going to be in Mexico for Christmas, so I bought Arianna a few small gifts, one of which was a ring. She had a ring on eight of her fingers and loved rings.

One night I was lying in bed, and I was thinking, *I have a ring for her. I should ask her to marry me.* So I put the ring in my jacket so I would have it with me on the plane. For the last month before we were to go, I was obsessed. That's all I talked about. All I thought about. All the things we would do while we were there.

I flew home on the sixteenth of December. I spent a few days with my family. We were leaving for Mexico on the nineteenth. Well, it was time. I'd been waiting for this for months now. We spent the night before we left at her house. My daughter took us to the airport the next morning. We were on the plane and on our way. I went and got the ring out of my jacket and sat down. I looked at Arianna eye to eye and said, "Arianna Bowater. I love you. Would you be my wife?"

She looked at me with a puzzled look, and before she could answer, I said, "There's only one catch. When we get on the plane to come home, we get a divorce."

Well, she started laughing and looked at me and said, "Andre, you know I love you. Of course I will be your wife!"

I put the ring on her finger. We were married. Married for ten days.

Not long after, I looked at her and said, "Arianna, I plan on making love to you a hundred times while we're on vacation."

She said, "But we're only going for ten days."

"I know!" I smiled at her. Then I said, "We'll count last night as number 100 and count down."

So it became an ongoing joke. The next will be 99 and so on. I can remember the night I looked at her and said, "Arianna, I can't wait for 87."

So we landed in Mexico, and Roberto was there holding up a sign with my name. Perfect. We got in his van, and he said, "Would you like a margarita?"

Arianna was too excited and mixed herself a drink. I had a beer. He gave us the gear he had picked up for us. We did a line. Welcome to Mexico.

On our way to the resort, he asked if we were hungry. "Sure," we replied.

So he pulled over to an authentic Mexican diner, and we ate authentic Mexican food. We got to the resort, and I handed him almost $900. It was $640 for the gear, and $200 for the ride to and from the resort. Then he told me that he found a girl we could spend the night with, but it was going to cost a thousand dollars. That's right! One thousand!

Arianna looked at me and said, "We don't need a girl that bad."

I met a guy here in McMoney who told me that he went to Mexico every set off in the winter, and he showed me a video of this girl he partied with. Five dollars for her company. Five freakin' dollars.

I looked at him and asked, "Did you have sex with her?"

"Of course I did," he replied

He partied and had sex with a girl for the day for five bucks. Here Roberto wanted a thousand for a girl for one night. The gear he got for us was not very good either. The shit I get in Canada was just as good. The Gs were rather small as well. He made off like a bandit. He basically took advantage of us. Big time. It's no wonder he didn't want any money from me for the Mexican food.

We got to the resort, checked in, and went to our room. We changed and went directly to the beach. We took a long walk on the beach and started back to our room. On the way back, there was a common area where there was a pool. Super busy during the day, not a soul around in the evening. We decided to go in. I stripped all my clothes off, and Arianna kept her panties and top on. Wow, what a feeling. To know there's snow and its cold at home, and here we were, in a pool in Mexico. She straddled her legs around me, and of course, I found my way inside her. Damn, life was good!

Just as I was thinking that very thought, this security dude came around the corner and told us to exit the pool. I tried everything. "But we just arrived two hours ago, and we're being very quiet," I said to him.

"No, you have to get out," he insisted.

Needless to say, I shrank until I was no longer inside her. Oyeoyeoye.

We went back to our room and did 98. We went out and around the resort. Had a bite to eat and went back to our room. We had a long day and decided to get some sleep.

When we got up, we went for breakfast, a massive buffet with everything you can imagine you could want for breakfast and more. We went back to our room to change and went to the beach. That was basically our routine for the first few days.

Anyways, we went to book a few excursions, and the dude looked at me and asked, "It's your birthday on Wednesday?"

"Yes, it is," I replied.

"Well, you should go to Coco Bongo."

I had promised Arianna's mom I would not take her daughter off the resort. I had also told Arianna we would not leave the resort (except for our excursions). I told her that if we went to a club and a cartel member saw her and wanted her, there was no way I would be able to protect her from that. Even if I was Schwarzenegger. Or even if I had a weapon. The cartel always get what they want.

The fellow proceeded to tell us that a bus would take us from the resort and bring us back. We watched the video of Coco Bongo. There was Spider-Man, flying in the air through the bar and other way cool stuff flying around. The music seemed to be awesome.

Arianna looked at me. I looked at her. We both nodded our heads and booked the excursion. After all, how bad could it be? Of course we forgot all the reasons not to leave the resort.

Wednesday came. We went for our a la carte dinner. We were looking good! I can remember thinking how I couldn't wait to remove that sexy skirt she was wearing. We had the waiter take a picture of us. I don't post on Facebook very often, but I went on and posted that picture of us, saying, "BEST BIRTHDAY EVER." Here I was turning sixty, and I was with a beautiful girl half my age. I felt like the luckiest man on the planet. I even told Arianna as much.

I had bought some blue pills from a friend before I left McMoney. I assumed they were Ecstasy. So we brought two of them and two caps of MDMA in case the pills weren't good enough. We took the pill as we got on the bus. When we got to Playa del Carmen, it was approximately nine thirty.

We got off the bus, and I looked at Arianna and said, "Mine is starting to kick in."

"Me too," she said.

"We're going to need some gum, aren't we?" I said.

She agreed, and as I was saying that, a street vendor walked directly in front of me. So I bought a pack. I took a piece, gave her a piece, and put the pack in her purse because my pockets were full. I started to chew the gum. We were maybe a hundred meters from the club. That's pretty well the last thing I remember.

We woke up the next day at five thirty in the afternoon. That's right. Twenty hours later. We didn't remember anything. We woke up and looked at each other with blank stares.

"What the hell happened last night?" Arianna asked.

"I don't know. What happened?"

I vaguely remember getting my bracelet put on my wrist and nothing more.

She looked at me and said, "Do you suppose the blue pill did that to us?"

"I don't think it would be the pill. Who would sell pills that make you black out? He wouldn't sell too many."

So we figured it had to be the gum. It was the last thing I remember doing, but if it was, it hit us some fast. My phone was gone, my credit card was gone, but ended up being at the front desk. My $2,000 gold chain was gone. I know, I'm an idiot for wearing it off the resort. My driver's license was in Arianna's purse, and her license was gone. Even the gum was gone from her purse. You don't realize how much you depend on your phone until you find yourself without it. We were lost. We didn't have contact with Roberto or anyone at home. The only number I knew by heart was my mother's. I couldn't get in my emails. To change my password, they wanted to send me a text on my phone.

I ended up contacting Travel Guru to get Roberto's contact information and what time we were leaving the following Wednesday. It didn't completely ruin the rest of our vacation, but it certainly didn't help. I had spent hours making up a playlist on Spotify for our beach party we planned on having. I couldn't take all the pictures I would have taken. I could go on and on, but I'll leave it at that.

We ran into one of the kids who was on the bus with us on the way to Coco Bongo, and he looked at us and said, "What the hell happened to you guys the other night? You guys were on drugs or something?" He said Arianna couldn't even hold her head up. He said that I could walk, but barely. He said I fell over and grabbed him on my way down, and he fell with me. That would explain the big scab I had on my head. He said ten, fifteen minutes later, we got kicked out of the club. They told us at the front desk that we had arrived at the resort at one thirty in the morning in a cab. So if we got kicked out of the club at ten o'clock and didn't arrive at the resort until one thirty, there's three and a half hours unaccounted for. So many things could have happened between ten and one thirty, and we didn't remember any of it. At least we didn't end up in jail—or worse dead. Tourists go missing in Mexico all the time.

Our beach party was a wash. I didn't have my phone and no playlist. We had to be close to Wi-Fi to play music on Arianna's phone and find songs to play one at a time. Oyeoyeoye

Well, the time had come for us to leave. It's never much fun when you know you're going back to reality. It was time to say farewell to Mexico. Until the next time.

Roberto came to pick us up and drove us to the airport. We were on the plane. It was sad. Sad to leave and sad to get a divorce. We were on our way home on the twenty-ninth of December, and Arianna looked at me and said, "What are you doing for New Year's?"

I answered, "Haven't you had enough of me already?"

We ended up hanging again for New Year's. Oh, and as for our countdown, we made it to 78. We made love twenty-two times in the ten days we were there. Minus 100 the night before we left, so twenty-one times in Mexico.

After coming home and talking to people, we were lucky to have come home at all. So many different scenarios could have happened. They could have slashed my throat, through me in the jungle, and kept Arianna as a sex slave. They could have sold her and got top dollar for her on the human trafficking market. We could have just disappeared. Can you imagine if I woke up that afternoon and Arianna wasn't in the room with me? I would still be there searching for her. There's no way I would take a woman on vacation anywhere and leave without her. I would have died there looking for her.

C h a p t e r   1 3

Breaking News

ARIANNA CAME TO VISIT ME IN MCMONEY a month ago, a year and a half after our trip. She wanted to see West Edmonton Mall, so I flew her in to Edmonton and took her to the mall. We spent the night in Edmonton. Then we drove home to McMoney.

So Friday night, we had planned on going to a new club that just opened in McMoney Club Rewind. It was a four-minute walk from my house. They played techno there, and we were going to go dancing. So we got cleaned up and decided to take one of those blue pills like we had taken in Mexico. It's been a year and a half since we went to Mexico. So you see, I'm not an addict. I didn't do any of the pills I had left.

Anyways, we took them around nine, and we were going to go to the club around ten o'clock. Well, my roommate was on night shift, and he came home at eight thirty the next morning and found me lying on the floor snoring like a bear. Then he heard noises coming from my en suite, so he knew Arianna was okay. Yes, you guessed it. It was the blue pill that made us black out in Mexico. Un-freakin'-believable. We didn't get drugged in Mexico. We did it to ourselves. Oyeoyeoye.

I wasn't going to tell y'all about the new development out of embarrassment, but hey. It is what it is. I had five of those pills left. I flushed four of them down the toilet and kept one to see if I could get a lab to test it, to see what the hell was in them to make us black out like that.

Arianna and I kept in touch. I loved her company and the way she made me feel when I was with her. It was almost like a drug or alcohol. When I was with her, the rest of the world did not exist.

Honorable Mentions

Now, let's touch on a few stories that are worth mentioning before I leave y'all.

Sprayer

One afternoon I was at work and decided to check out the vine to see who might be on there. I started talking to this young girl. We were having fun chatting, so we decided to meet up at Timmy's. I got to Timmy's, and she was there waiting for me. She came over to my car and got in. We both had things to do that afternoon, but had decided to meet beforehand.

She had shoulder-length blonde hair and was fairly attractive. We chatted for a bit and decided we should hang out sometime. We made arrangements to meet up, and we got ready to leave. She got out of my car and looked at me and said, "By the way, I'm commando right now."

I thought about what she just told me and started getting an erection, thinking about how she's not wearing any panties, how I could rip her pants off and fuck her right there in my car. *Okay, Andre. You both have things to do. Later for the sex.*

She left me there with my erection and went on her way.

Later that week, I went to her place to hang out. Or should I say, I went there to fuck her. We chatted for a few minutes, then I had to see if she was still commando. Sure enough, no panties. She grabbed me by the sides of my head and directed me toward her pussy. I licked and gently bit her clit. We had sex, then lay there and chatted. I ended up standing up on her bed and aimed at her mouth and went in. I pounded her face for like fifteen to twenty minutes. I eventually came in her mouth. Damn, it feels good when you can push it all in without that gag reflex that a lot of women have. I can't even describe the feeling when your head penetrates the throat of a woman. She was an amazing sex partner.

So we're lying there chatting, and she told me how she found out how to make herself squirt (she called it spraying). She looked at me and asked if I wanted to watch while she showed me.

"Sure, I'm kinda curious as to how you're going to do this."

She stood up beside the bed and put two of her fingers inside and started going in and out. All of a sudden, she said, "Watch. Watch!" She starts spraying.

I will admit, it was fun to watch. She finished up, and we chatted for a while before I left. I called her a few times after that and never got an answer. The last time I called,

I never got an answer, and right after that call, I received a call from the RCMP. They told me to stop calling her because she didn't want to talk to me. I told them that all she had to do was tell me she didn't want to talk to me, and I would have stopped calling. Not sure what caused her to feel that way, but there are too many fish in the sea for me to get hung up on her. Oyeoye!

Two Crackers

Not all Grapevine encounters were good ones. I met one chick off the vine one night in Edmonton. I went to meet her, and she had a roommate who was pretty hot. We left to get a hotel room, and on the way, I convinced her to contact her roommate to see if she would come with us. She called, and her roommate said she would join us.

So we turned around and went back to get her. Perfect! I was getting a hotel room to have sex with two women.

We got to the hotel, and they were acting kinda weird. I thought nothing of it.

We went in and hung out, chatting for a bit. I then went in the room with the one chick I had originally met. I banged her for ten or fifteen minutes, then I called the other one in. I banged her for the same ten or fifteen minutes. I figured I should save myself for the first one (as she was bigger than, her friend and I didn't want her to be jealous). I was blowing my load as she started going on about me fucking her friend. How I liked her friend more than I liked her. Next thing I knew, they were asking me for money, saying if I didn't give them money, they were going to call the cops and have me arrested.

Well, I wasn't long getting the fuck out of there. I'm not sure how they got home, but I didn't care at that point. I just wanted to get out of dodge. I'm pretty sure they were smoking crack. They were smoking while I was having sex with one and then changing. Either way, I had fun while it lasted. I wasn't about to let two women I didn't know threaten me for money. So that was the end of that adventure.

How Good

So I was in Edmonton one night, and I was bored and horny. I went on the vine and started chatting with this girl. She was looking for someone who was willing to be generous. I was bored and horny. So sure I'll be generous.

She told me what she was looking to get for sex, and I agreed. I was on my way to her house, and I got her on the phone. We were talking, and I told her how I wanted to taste her. Well, she piped up and told me that if I wanted to taste, it was going to cost me more money. I didn't take that well and told her I wasn't willing to give her any more than we had agreed on, especially to do something that she would enjoy. She told me it was going to be more. So I changed my mind and went home. I was not a big fan of paying for sex to begin with.

A few weeks later, I found her on the vine, and we started chatting again. I went to her place, and we met. She was pretty freakin' hot. I was a good boy, and instead of trying to have sex with her, I asked her if she would like to go to the mountains with me for a night or two. She told me that she was busy with work, but she would make time to go with me for one night. I made the arrangements and told her when we could go. We were going to go on a Saturday for the night and return Sunday.

I took off from McMoney Saturday morning to go to Edmonton to get her. She jumped in my car, and I was thinking she was hot. I couldn't wait to fuck her. After all, I should have already had sex with her.

We were going to Jasper. When we arrived, we went to our hotel and got settled in, went for supper, and got ready to go for a few drinks and go dancing. I love Jasper because it's not as touristy as Banff, and there was a club there that played techno. We went out and danced our asses off and got pretty drunk.

When we got back to our room, she started looking for her hash to have a puff. She couldn't remember where it was, and she was pissed off. I don't know if she thought I had hidden her hash or what, but she ended up going to bed. I blame the alcohol for that kind of behavior. Well, I guess I was not getting any sex tonight…again. Oyeoyeoye.

I let her calm down and went and lay beside her. I slowly reached over and started touching her. She didn't resist, so I started to remove her panties. She rolled over and parted her legs. I guess that was my invitation to come in. I climbed on top of her and went in. Oh my god! How good her vagina felt wrapped around my member. How much better it feels when you don't think it's going to hap-pen, and it does. I didn't want to push my luck, so I didn't get to taste her. But I was happy just to have gotten inside her. It was definitely an awesome way to finish a night of fun and dancing.

We got up the next morning, and she found her hash almost right away. We went for breakfast and hung out for a bit, talking about how much fun we had at the club. We went back to our room to pack and got ready to head home. On our way home, we stopped at a touristy type place and took a few pictures. Not long after that weekend, she met a man and got into a relationship, so we didn't communicate much after that.

The Professional

Another time, back home in Halifax, I was on the vine, and I heard this message from what sounded like an attractive lady. On her greeting, she was giving her measurements, age, and what she was looking for. So I sent her a message. As you know, some women on the vine want men who are willing to be generous, meaning they want money for sex. I did not really have a problem with that as long as they were attractive enough for me to want to pay. After all, there were a lot of women on the vine who were barely scraping by. They just needed a little extra money and were willing to have sex for cash. In my opinion, prostitution is the oldest profession in the world. As long as there are men on the planet, there will always be men who are willing to pay for a vagina. So if you have a vagina, you might as well try to get money for the use of it. So they enjoy getting fucked, and they can make a few bucks doing it.

Back to chicky. We started to chat, and she told me where she lived and asked me if I would be generous. She told me what she charged. She sounded like someone I may not mind paying to have sex with, so I went to meet her.

Well, I got there, and she lived next door to one of the places Cathy used to live in. I remember going to visit (fuck) Cathy and her telling me that she thought the girl living next door to her was a prostitute. Cathy told me that there were men coming and going at all hours of the day and night.

Well, sure enough, she was right. Cathy had moved away from there months before I went there that night. So I knocked on the door. She opened the door, and I was like…WTF! She was hot as fuck. I was thinking I would definitely pay to fuck her.

She invited me in. We started to chat, and I was trying to convince her that she should come down south with me for ten days. I told her I would pay for her trip, and we could get away for a while and enjoy each other's company. There was nothing I could say to convince her. I know she liked me because she told me so. She more or less told me that she was a sex addict, and she wasn't going anywhere with anyone. She told me that she didn't really drink or do drugs. Her addiction was to have sex. I still can't, to this day, believe what happened that evening.

Well, like I said previously in this book, I can't wait to die to relive the sexual experience I had with her. We made out like schoolkids, my tongue down her throat, and she loved it. She was a great kisser. We did oral on each other like it was a professional sport. She tasted so fresh and so good. She loved receiving and giving. She was extremely good at it as well.

I still can't believe that she never made me wear a condom, which maybe I should have, but bareback always feels so much better. Well then, we had sex, the best sex I had ever had and will probably ever have. She was very vocal. She was the best at every event and challenge we took on. I most definitely will say that being with her was the best sexual experience I have ever had. She had it all, and she was a gold medalist at every event. I have been with a few escorts and never once thought about kissing them or not wearing a condom. She was very attractive, had an amazing body. She was the whole package and some.

On my way to her place, I had stopped at the bank and took out enough money for a half hour of her time. When I got ready to leave, she told me I owed her for an hour. I only had enough to pay her for a half hour, and she was not happy. I tried to tell her I would bring her more money later, but she was angry. I ended up leaving, feeling disappointed in myself for not bringing more money with me. I have never gone back to see her, but I think about her every time I go home to Halifax.

After reliving that moment with you, I have decided that the next time I go home, I will have to go see if she still lives there. I want to fuck her again so badly, I can taste it. I haven't paid for sex very often in my life, but boy…she was worth every penny I gave her and more. She may have been a prostitute, but she wasn't a street walker. She was a pro, and she knew what she wanted. She wanted to get fucked, and she loved it. After all, how many prostitutes will let you kiss them? How many prostitutes will give you oral sex and not make you wear a condom? How many will let you fuck them without a condom? She is likely one of the very few. She was definitely one of a kind.

Mean Dog

One afternoon, I was at McDonald's having supper, and I went on the vine. I started chatting with a lady who lived five minutes away. I told her I was just finishing up supper. She asked me if I could get a Big Mac for her and come over. So of course, I aim to please. I got her burger and headed over to her place.

She was a few years younger than me and was pretty good-looking. She had two dogs, one of which she said she had rescued from the SPCA. This dog was very aggressive and kept jumping up on her. He was scratching her legs repeatedly. He would not listen to her. I didn't much like him and would have taken him back in a heartbeat, but I was only there for a short time anyways.

I helped her with a few projects she was having problems with. She was doing small renovations. We hung out, and turned out I knew her brother. She thanked me for my help. She went to her room and didn't seem to be coming back. She called my name and asked me to come join her in her bedroom.

We climbed in her bed, and she took charge. She started giving me oral, and my god, it felt unbelievable. I could tell that she loved what she was doing. She went on and on. By far, one of the best BJs I ever had besides the professional. I eventually jumped on top and penetrated her as I was looking at her face. I love to look at my partner's face as I'm pushing myself inside her. It's one of my fetishes.

When I was done, we lay in bed for a while. All of a sudden, she reached over and grabbed my penis and started playing with me to make me hard. She started giving me oral again. She loved giving oral, and I was not going to stop her. Oyeoyeoye.

Before I left her house, I made the mistake of telling her that she should correct her new dog's behavior, or he would never stop. She got very defensive. She was very offended and basically told me to mind my own business.

So that didn't end on a good note. I regret giving her my opinion as I may have been able to become better friends with her. I love oral when it feels that good. A woman who likes giving oral that feels that amazing is a rarity. Plus, she was a very nice lady.

A Smelly Affair

So there was this woman on POF I had been trying to chat with. I messaged her a few times, and she never replied. One night I messaged her again and ended up going to EVP for a few drinks. I was at the bar and started chatting with the fellow sitting beside me. Meanwhile, there were these two hotties sitting behind us. Buddy I was chatting with was a pretty good-looking dude, and I was thinking, *We can probably pick these chickies up.*

One of the girls got up and went to the bathroom. Her girlfriend got up and started dancing at the table. It was in the last stages of COVID, and people hadn't been dancing for a few years now with all the social distancing crap and all. There was my opportunity.

I walked on over and said, "It's been a while since I had a dance. Are you having fun?"

She replied, "I know, it has been a while."

We started chatting, and we had a few things in common. By the time her girlfriend came back, we were hitting it off. I offered the girls to have a shot, and they came over to the bar, and we proceeded to have a shot, the four of us. Okay, so far, so good.

All of a sudden, I hear *bleep bleep*! I looked at my phone, and it was the chick I had been trying to chat with for weeks on POF. I messaged her, and she wanted to come join me at the bar. Oye. *What do I do?* Well, I had a decision to make. This girl I was messaging sounded like she wanted to get laid. *Okay, well…do I stay and see where it will go with these two girls? Or do I go for the sure thing and go pick this girl up?*

So I decided to go pick her up. We were chatting on the phone, and she decided she would rather hang out, just the two of us. So I went to the liquor store and headed over to her place. I got there and went in, and we started to chat. There were two dogs at her place, and the place smelled like a kennel (remind you of anything?). We chatted for a few minutes, and I convinced her to come to my place. We got there, and I put some music on, and I was singing and dancing, and she was like "Oh my god, you're fuckin' awesome. Where have you been all my life? I can't wait to rape you."

She kept repeating those three lines over and over. She had her hair up in a ponytail, and I knew what that usually meant—they haven't washed their hair. So I said to her, "You should go in the shower and wash up, and I'll be in bed naked waiting for you when you get out."

"No, I'm all right," she said.

Ten to fifteen minutes later, I mentioned the shower again, and she insisted she was okay. We had a few drinks and eventually made our way to the bedroom. We played around for ten or fifteen minutes, then I jumped on top of her and pounded her in to tomorrow. When we were done, I could smell her pussy. Pussy had a pleasant smell. They all smell the same if they smell at all, but this smell was rather strong. We chatted for a bit until I reloaded, and I jumped on top of her again. Well, by the time I was done the second time, I could barely stand the putrid smell in my room. It was horrible. The worst I ever experienced. It took me a while before I could go to sleep; the smell was so strong. I eventually fell asleep.

I woke up through the night to have a pee, and it smelled so bad that it took me another half hour or more to go back to sleep.

We got up the next morning, and she went in the living room and had a seat. I proceeded to rip the sheets off my bed and throw them in the wash while she was watching. It's always fun to get laid, but in this case, I had to think. I would have rather brought those two young hotties home and partied with them, even if I didn't have sex with them, than go through what happened. Oh my god. I was awesome. Where had I been all her life? She couldn't wait to rape me. Oyeoyeoye. We could have turned out to be best fuck buddies, but after that, *no, thank you.* Maybe she should have taken me up on that offer to have a shower. *Next.*

Nothing Ventured

This story is too cute not to put in as a grand finale. So when the fires hit Fort McMoney, I had flown home a week earlier to meet my new grandson. My house burnt down while I was away. I was grateful I wasn't in McMoney to experience the evacuation. It was a nightmare.

Anyways, I started talking to a woman from McMoney on POF or Tinder. We exchanged phone numbers and started chatting on the phone. She had evacuated to a campground near Grassland that her brother owned. We were getting to know each other pretty good when I had this crazy idea that we should go to Canada's Wonderland. As you know, I love coasters. She was in Grassland, Alberta, and I was in Halifax, Nova Scotia. Practically across the country from each other.

I asked her if she liked roller coasters and amusement park rides. She said she used to, but hadn't been in years.

"Mary Anne," I said, "what would you say if we flew to Toronto and met. Then we could go to Wonderland together?"

After giving it some thought, she decided that was a pretty good idea. I told her that if we didn't feel it after we met, we could sleep in separate beds and just enjoy each other's company.

"Let's go to Wonderland and have some fun."

She agreed.

It sounded like a good idea. I told her that all she had to pay for was her airfare, and I would pay for everything else. That's right, she flew from Edmonton to Toronto to meet a complete stranger. Doing something like that is riskier for a woman than a man.

I flew from Halifax, and we were to meet for the first time in Toronto.

On fly day, I arrived in Toronto. I called her and asked her where she was so I could come meet her. She told me that she was getting our rental car at Avis.

"Come meet me here," she said.

I got my bag and went off to Avis. I got there, and I was sneaking around so that I could see her before she saw me. I couldn't see her anywhere, so I called her back.

She said, "Where are you?"

"At Avis," I replied.

"No, you're not. I'm in the office finishing up the paperwork, and I don't see you anywhere. Which terminal are you at?" she asked.

Well, it turned out I was at the wrong terminal. We finally met up, and I gave her a big hug, and I was thinking, *I hope she likes me half as much as I like her.* Even though I said I would pay for everything, she ended up paying for the rental car and a few other things.

Off we went and headed for Wonderland. We got there and found a hotel. We got settled in. We still had enough time to start our adventure and went to get a bite to eat. After that, we went straight to the park. We walked around the park and checked out the new rides. When we got back to our room after a long day of travel and time at the park, I could tell that she kinda liked me, but when she climbed into bed with me, I knew.

We started touching and kissing. We had sex. It's such an amazing feeling when you have sex for the first time with someone. But it's also a little awkward breaking the ice with a new partner.

So the plan was that we would go to the park the next day, and when we left there, we would go to my sister's for the night. My sister lived fifteen minutes from Wonderland. Then we were going to go to Niagara Falls for one night, then go back to Toronto for one more day at the park.

We had a great day at the park. She was intimidated by the rides and was apprehensive about joining me. We had a fun day nonetheless. At the end of the day, we went for something to eat. Then we went to my sister's to hang out for a few hours. We eventually went to bed. I slowly and quietly climbed on top of her, and we said good night with our bodily fluids.

The next day, we took off for Niagara. Before we arrived, we went online and found a room for us to stay in. When we arrived, we checked in, and when we went in our room, you will never guess what was in our room. Beside the bed, there was a red heart-shaped hot tub. Are you kidding me? Three feet from our bed. I had brought two Ecstasy pills just in case I could convince her to take one with me. She wasn't into drugs, but she agreed to do one with me that night. We did the pill and went to a techno club. We didn't end up staying there for long because the DJ wasn't playing very good music, and she didn't like it. So we ended up going back to our room.

On the way back to our room, it was freakin' hot out that night, and the buzz from the pill made me even hotter. I decided to take my shirt off to cool down. She started telling me to put my shirt back on. One thing led to another, and by the time we got back to the room, she was angry with me. I wasn't doing anything illegal or breaking the law in any way. We went in to the room, and she climbed in bed.

I wasn't going to sleep three feet away from a hot tub without getting into it. I filled the tub and jumped in. Alone. Oye. I'm pretty good at fucking things up sometimes. But I'm not very good at fixing them. I really didn't do much to make her angry. I just refused to put my shirt back on.

We got up the next morning like nothing had happened. I'm not sure why she reacted that way the night before. Maybe the fact that she was high and wasn't sure how to handle the high…maybe. I don't know. At least she wasn't holding a grudge, and the day went on as if nothing had happened. That's how most situations like that should be. What good is it to hold a grudge over something as trivial as that?

I'm just like that. I don't like anger. Anger is one of those emotions that does not let go. If you don't get over it, it's like cancer. It festers and grows inside of you. It can make you say or do things you end up regretting. So I applaud her.

We went back to Toronto the next day and went back to the park. We had a lot of fun together, and I really liked her company. We slept at our hotel that night, and everything was fine. If you know what I mean. Although that was the last time we were ever intimate. The plan had been that we would fly back to Edmonton together. Reentry to McMoney was a few days later, and I had a condo meeting to attend. She offered to let me to stay at her place with her. She had a spare room for me to use in her condo. She's a nice lady, and we still chat occasionally. We made some good memories.

Just a quickie, while I was staying with Mary Anne, I got a message from a young girl on Tinder. She wanted to come to my place and wanted me to fuck her. I told her the timing was bad, and I couldn't make that happen. My house had burned down, and I was just trying to find my vehicle that one of my boarders had saved from the fire.

Missed opportunity. Oyeoye.

Well, I hope you enjoyed these stories. I have often told the odd story at work when we're bored or when hanging out. People get a charge at my boldness. How carefree and funny I am. I was often told, "That's funny as hell. You should write a book."

I went for lunch with a friend and told him and a friend of his one of these stories. He looked at me and said, "That's funny as hell. You should write a book."

I went home and thought, *Do I have enough stories to actually write a book?* I thought of this one and that one and decided I had enough stories, and it was time to write this book. So here we are. I had a lot of fun writing about these experiences. It was like I was reliving those memories of my past. I found myself going to the bathroom a few times though. LOL. You don't even know how many times I wanted to add "LOL" to some of the lines in this book. I'm sure if you made it this far that you got the humor I portrayed in these stories.

This was a one-time deal. Don't be expecting another book from me. I'm not going to be alive long enough to experience those kinds of crazy situations and experiences.

The reason I named the book *A Much Better Life* is that I have had a much better life since my divorce than before my marriage. My life is nothing like before I was married. Life is full of opportunities if you see the glass half-full. I hope you found the humor in the book and picked up on the subtle hints that can make your life more enjoyable.

For the record, not long after Arianna's visit to McMoney, I decided that I was going to stop doing drugs. I'm getting older, and I don't enjoy it as much as I once did. I haven't done drugs in a little over two years now. It had always been a social thing for me anyways. Besides, I haven't been in any type of a relationship in ten plus years. It's time to buckle up and find myself a lady to enjoy my retirement with. As a result of my new drug free life. Arianna and I have parted ways.

Thank you.